The CHRISTIAN Home

CLARENCE SEXTON

STUDENT HANDBOOK

CROWN
PUBLICATIONS
Royal Reading

The CHRISTIAN Home

CLARENCE SEXTON

SECOND EDITION
COPYRIGHT
MAY 2003

1700 BEAVER CREEK DRIVE
POWELL, TENNESSEE ♦ 37849
1-877 AT CROWN
www.FaithfortheFamily.com

SUNDAY SCHOOL SERIES

THE CHRISTIAN HOME

Copyright © 2001, 2003
Crown Publications
Powell, Tennessee 37849
ISBN: 1-58981-064-3
Layout and design by Stephen Troell

Cover painting, *Light to the Gentiles* © Greg Olsen.
By arrangement with Mill Pond Press, Inc. Venice, FL 34292
For information on art prints by Greg Olsen, please contact
Mill Pond Press at 1-800-535-0331.

Printed in the United States of America

This book is affectionately dedicated to my precious wife and most cherished friend — Evelyn!

"Her children arise up, and call her blessed."
Her church family numbers her among the "Holy women."

Her grandchildren see "the beauty of the LORD" upon her.
"The heart of her husband doth safely trust in her."

Clarence Burton
Acts 5:42

Table of Contents

*"And whatsoever ye do in word or deed,
do all in the name of the Lord Jesus,
giving thanks to God and the Father by him.
Wives, submit yourselves unto your own
husbands, as it is fit in the Lord. Husbands,
love your wives, and be not bitter against
them. Children, obey your parents in all
things: for this is well pleasing unto the
Lord. Fathers, provoke not your children
to anger, lest they be discouraged."*

Colossians 3:17-21

Chapter One

Determine to Have a Christian Home

 house is a place, but a home is made of people. A Christian home is a home where people are living their Christian faith each day.

I recently had the privilege of talking to a man who builds houses. He took me on a tour of some of the houses he had built. As we went from house to house, he explained that there were different grades of materials that could be used to build each house.

The cost of the house depended on the quality of the material used. The dwelling with the least expensive material was just as much a "house" as the building with the most expensive material. They were built for the same purpose; the only difference was in the quality of the materials that were used. Simply stated, it costs more to have a better house because of the

quality of the materials. Many people appear to be working hard on their home life but are simply using the wrong materials.

The Bible says in the book of Colossians, chapter three, verses fifteen through twenty-one, *"And let the peace of God rule in your hearts, to the which also ye are called in one body; and be ye thankful. Let the word of Christ dwell in you richly in all wisdom; teaching and admonishing one another in psalms and hymns and spiritual songs, singing with grace in your hearts to the Lord. And whatsoever ye do in word or deed, do all in the name of the Lord Jesus, giving thanks to God and the Father by him. Wives, submit yourselves unto your own husbands, as it is fit in the Lord. Husbands, love your wives, and be not bitter against them. Children, obey your parents in all things: for this is well pleasing unto the Lord. Fathers, provoke not your children to anger, lest they be discouraged."*

> *A house is a place, but a home is made of people. A Christian home is a home where people are living their Christian faith each day.*

THREE HOMES WE ALL NEED

We all should have three homes. We need to know that we have a heavenly home. If we have asked the Lord to forgive our sin, and by faith we have received the Lord Jesus Christ; we have a heavenly home.

We should have a good church home. Do not underestimate the power and influence of a good, Bible-believing, Bible-preaching church. Everyone should believe on the Lord Jesus Christ as Savior and belong to a Bible-believing, Bible-preaching church. We know that Jesus Christ is the foundation and the head of the church, but we cannot have strong churches without strong families. If we turn the coin to the other side, we find that what strengthens the home is a good Bible-believing, Bible-preaching church. We need a good church home.

Not only do we need a heavenly home and a church home, but we also need a strong Christian home. Satan is real, and families are falling apart everywhere. I hope these thoughts from God's Word will strengthen you and your family as you determine to have a Christian home.

WHAT MAKES A HOME CHRISTIAN?

Many who claim to be Christians do not have a Christian home. There are some people who have a clear Christian testimony of their salvation, but they do not have a Christian home.

What makes a home Christian? You may say, "My husband is a Christian. Doesn't that make my home Christian?" No, not necessarily. You may say, "The mother of the home is a Christian. Doesn't that make it a Christian home?" You may even attend church faithfully, but none of these things make a home Christian.

> *Not only do we need a heavenly home and a church home, but we also need a strong Christian home.*

If you will consider the context of the family in the passage of Scripture in Colossians chapter three, you will discover the ingredients of a Christian home. In Colossians 3:12-13 seven things are given in a list. Consider them carefully: *"Put on therefore, as the elect of God, holy and beloved, bowels of mercies, kindness, humbleness of mind, meekness, longsuffering; forbearing one another, and forgiving one another..."*

After giving these seven things, the Lord covers them with the overcoat of Christian love. *"And above all these things put on charity, which is the bond of perfectness."* We are given the clothing of the Christian life with the overcoat of Christian love.

THE INGREDIENTS OF A CHRISTIAN HOME

PEACE

"And let the peace of God rule in your hearts."

A truly Christian home is a place of peace with the peace of God ruling in people's hearts. It is not a battleground, but a refuge. It is not a place of fighting, but a place of fellowship. It is a place fortified against the Devil.

In God's Word, we read about peace *with* God and the peace *of* God.

Jesus Christ was sent forth to earth, and He gave Himself on the cross. He bled and died for our sins, tasting death for every man. God punished sin in the body of His own Son when He became sin for us. He died, was buried, and rose from the dead. When we ask Him to forgive our sin and by faith receive Him as our Savior, we are born into God's family. We become children of God, and we have peace with God.

However, having peace *with* God does not mean that we have the peace *of* God. Look closely at a passage of Scripture in Philippians 4:5-7,

> *Let your moderation be known unto all men. The Lord is at hand. Be careful for nothing; but*

in every thing by prayer and supplication with thanksgiving let your requests be made known unto God. And the peace of God, which passeth all understanding, shall keep your hearts and minds through Christ Jesus.

The world cannot understand this peace. Psalm 119:165 says, *"Great peace have they which love thy law: and nothing shall offend them."* This means that nothing blows them off course. The world cannot understand this kind of peace.

If your home is a place of battling and fighting, it is not a Christian home according to the standard of God's Word. You may be a worker in the church and still not have a Christian home. A Christian home is a place where the peace of God rules.

THANKFULNESS

"And let the peace of God rule in your hearts, to the which also ye are called in one body; and be ye thankful."

In a Christian home we find thankfulness. It is so easy to become ungrateful. It is so easy to gripe and complain. We desire everything to be right. We want everyone to live right and do right. We allow ourselves to become critical, and criticism is contagious. It leads to an ungrateful spirit.

In a Christian home, people do not gripe about what they have to eat; they thank God they have something to eat. They do not gripe about what they have to wear; they thank God they have something to wear. They do not murmur and complain all the time about one family member or another; they just thank God that they are all still alive, living under the same roof and enjoying one another's company. Be thankful for the time that you are together as a family on this earth. Enjoy it.

When you come to the end of life, those days you wasted are gone. How many of those days would you like to get back at the end? No one will get any of them back. A Christian home is ruled by the peace of God, and it is a place of thankfulness.

THE WORD OF GOD

"Let the word of Christ dwell in you richly in all wisdom."

The Bible says in Ecclesiastes 10:10, *"Wisdom is profitable to direct."* Many homes do not have God's direction because they do not have the Word of God dwelling in them richly. You do not have a Christian home if you do not have it full of the Bible. Hide God's Word in your heart. Place Bible verses and Bible plaques on the walls.

Take the time to read the Bible with your family. Emphasize the things of God. This will help you and your children as you seek to rear them for the glory of God. Take time to read God's Word, and pray with your family each day.

Many say they have a Christian home, but if these ingredients: peace, thankfulness, and the Word of God are not found, then we cannot call it a Christian home. These ingredients may seem simple, but they make a world of difference.

THE INSTRUCTION IN A CHRISTIAN HOME

What are we trying to teach in our homes? The Bible says in Colossians 3:16-17, *"Teaching and admonishing one another in psalms and hymns and spiritual songs, singing with grace in your hearts to the Lord. And whatsoever ye do in word or deed, do all in the name of the Lord Jesus, giving thanks to God and the Father by him."*

The Bible says we are to be *"teaching and admonishing."* To admonish means to counsel against wrong practices. It means to caution or advise people. We are to be *"teaching and admonishing one another in psalms and hymns and spiritual songs."*

CHRIST-HONORING MUSIC

Every beautiful Christian family that I have witnessed has a home where there is Christian music that honors the Lord. Families need to sing together. We have allowed the television to keep the family from coming together. We have found so many things to do that we have no time for one another.

You may think your child has everything he needs in his room. He may have his own television, phone, stereo, and headphones; but you have no idea what he is doing, listening to, or watching. This is the most ridiculous thing Christian parents could possibly do for their children. Your children should never listen to music in your home that you cannot hear or have not personally approved.

> *Every beautiful Christian family that I have witnessed has a home where there is Christian music that honors the Lord.*

I understand that this sounds old-fashioned, but we need some old-fashioned Christian homes. What do we teach in the home? We should be teaching hymns and spiritual songs. We should be singing and making melody in our hearts to the Lord. The Bible says, *"Singing with grace in your hearts to the Lord."*

THE LOVE OF CHRIST

"And whatsoever ye do in word or deed...."

There is a difference between *"word"* and *"deed."* People say, "I am against adultery," and then laugh at some television program that promotes it. Your children are watching you. You just taught them that it is not so bad after all.

You say that you are against ugly language, but you sit and watch it with your children on the television and laugh at the filthy jokes. The children say, "Daddy really isn't against ugly things, is he?" You say, "No alcohol." Then the beer commercials come on, and your children see you laughing. You just taught your children by deed that it is not so bad after all. It is one thing to say it, but it is another thing to live it.

> *You can get rid of anything dirty and wicked in your life; but if you do not have the love of Christ in your home, it is still not a Christian home.*

You should not do anything you do not want your children doing. You should not watch anything you do not want your children watching. I hear some people say, "Well, I am an adult; I can handle some of this stuff." You cannot handle it for very long. If you allow these things to come through your eye gate and ear gate long enough, they are going to have a detrimental effect on your life.

You can get rid of the television. You can eliminate bad habits. You can get rid of anything dirty and wicked in your life; but if you do not have the love of Christ in your home, it is still not a Christian home. Certain things should be removed, but the Christian home is determined more by what goes into it than what is taken out of it.

ACCOUNTABILITY TO CHRIST

"And whatsoever ye do in word or deed, do all in the name of the Lord Jesus."

Teach your children that we are all accountable to Christ. Mom and Dad must answer to the Lord, and the children must also answer to the Lord. There are times when you are not at your house and your children are alone. What are they going to do when you are not there? If you have taught them to be accountable to Christ, they will eventually realize that even when parents are not present, they must answer to the Lord.

There is a difference between good motives and the best motives. For example, a mother and father may live for their children. They may dedicate their whole lives to them. That is a good motive, but did you know that there is a higher motive? The best motive is to do what we do for Christ.

When what our children want and what Christ wants come into conflict, we should choose what the Lord wants over what they want. When we do that, we teach them that being accountable to Christ is more important than anything else. Children must come face to face with their own personal accountability to Christ.

Not only does a Christian home have ingredients, a Christian home has instruction. The instruction comes down to our personal accountability to Christ. The Bible says that every man shall give an account of himself to God. Instruct your family to live knowing that each day we all are accountable to God.

THE INDIVIDUALS
IN A CHRISTIAN HOME

WIVES

"Wives, submit yourselves unto your own husbands, as it is fit in the Lord."

God has a word for every individual in the Christian home. For the wife, the word that God gives is *"submit."* We will not stray far from what the word *"submit"* means if we think of the word *serve*. We learn from Ephesians chapter five that we are to submit to one another. The wife is to serve the husband, and the husband is to serve the wife. The wife is to submit to her husband, and the husband is to submit to his wife. There is mutual submission in our loving care for one another, but the wife is to submit to her husband's leadership.

No woman can ever make a man completely happy. It is ridiculous for a man to think that he can find complete fulfillment in a woman, for if he could, he would have no need of Christ. However, if you rear your children in a home where a wife does not submit to her husband, then your daughters will become wives who will not submit to their husbands. A wife who is not submissive teaches rebellion to her children by her behavior. This is not only a sin against your husband and the Lord, it is a sin against your children.

There are many women who should say, "God allowed me to be born a woman. God gave me a husband. Because God commands me to submit, I am going to submit." Your husband may not be all that he should be, but God's word for a woman in a Christian home is *"submit."* If you have a wife who is a Christian but does not submit, you do not have a Christian home.

HUSBANDS

The Bible says in verse nineteen, *"Husbands, love your wives, and be not bitter against them."* The word for the husband is *"love."*

Love is a commitment. It is possible for a man to be so committed to his wife that he does not allow his eyes to wander because he loves his wife and is committed to her. You can be a Christian man and be married; but if you do not love your wife even as Christ also loved the church and gave Himself for it, you do not have a Christian home. Loving our wives *"as Christ also loved the church"* means to make the commitment to them that He has made to the church, *"I will never leave thee, nor forsake thee"* (Hebrews 13:5).

> *You can be a Christian man and be married; but if you do not love your wife even as Christ also loved the church and gave Himself for it, you do not have a Christian home.*

CHILDREN

The Lord has a word for everyone. The Bible says, *"Children, obey your parents in all things: for this is well pleasing unto the Lord."* The word God gives to children is *"obey."* Wives are to submit, husbands are to love, and children are to obey.

Children are to honor and obey their parents. Honor has to do with attitude, and obedience has to do with action. As children become older, there is a conflict between becoming adults and obeying Mom and Dad. Our counsel to them is that as long as they depend on Mom and Dad for sustenance (money), they need to obey them. Children are to obey their parents. After they become adults, they are to honor them all the days of their lives.

FATHERS

Notice that God did not stop after this word to the children. He says, *"Fathers, provoke not your children to anger, lest they be discouraged."* How do fathers provoke their children? They can provoke a child with unrealistic expectations. There are no perfect children, yet so many people make such foolish mistakes by placing their children on high pedestals. Children should not be forced to live under unrealistic expectations.

> *Allow your children to get over their mistakes; do not continually remind them of their failures.*

We want our children to do right. We want them to live under right standards. Do not give in, and do not run all over the country talking about how wonderful your children are. Why? When people meet them they should say, "This girl or boy is even better than I expected."

Sometimes men and women relive their failures through their children. They want their children to try to be everything that they have not been. The Bible says, *"Fathers, provoke not your children."*

Fathers provoke their children by hypocrisy. Your children know what you are. Children lose confidence in their parents when they talk out of both sides of their mouths. When parents wear a mask and pretend to be something they are not, the children know it. This provokes children to anger and discourages them.

Fathers can provoke their children by having an unforgiving spirit. Allow your children to get over their mistakes; do not continually remind them of their failures. "Look what you did the last time. We have always had this kind of problem out of you." This is the wrong way to talk to your children. The Bible says, *"Fathers, provoke not your children to anger, lest they be discouraged."* God connects anger and discouragement; angry children become discouraged children. Anger driven inward produces discouragement. May the Lord help us to be the parents our children deserve to have.

Children should obey, but fathers should not provoke them. Wives should submit, but husbands must love them. We each need to say, "Lord, help me."

Our time on earth is so short, and our families are so precious. Our time with our families will pass quickly. When I hear about a family

> *Our time on earth is so short, and our families are so precious. Our time with our families will pass quickly. When I hear about a family that will not forgive a child, it breaks my heart.*

that will not forgive a child, it breaks my heart. The child can never go home; he cannot celebrate Christmas, birthday parties, or any other special family event. When the home is disrupted and there is such anger and unforgiveness, no one wins. May God help us.

My wife suggested to me when our children were still very young that we read through the Bible with them. I thought that getting them together and having them sit and listen would be an impossible task. I sort of had the idea that I was going to say,

"Sit down over here and I am going to read the Bible through to you. I can read it through in sixty hours. We will let you have a little orange juice between sessions. We are going to read until we're through." That is not how it happened. It happened about fifteen or twenty minutes every morning until we got through all 1,189 chapters of the Bible. This way we were able to go through the entire Bible many times with our children during their years at home. We went through every word of it again and again. We had Bible reading and prayer for a brief time each morning and a Bible story before bedtime at night. As they got older, they were expected to replace the Bible story at night with their own personal Bible reading; but we continued to pray with them and send them off to sleep with a hug. We have had so many failures, but there were things that we said we would take the time to do because they were right. We desired to have a Christian home.

Be sure you have trusted the Lord Jesus Christ as your Savior and seek God's help in having a Christian home.

Home Work

♦ Make your home a place of peace, not a battleground.

♦ Eliminate murmuring and complaining from your home.

♦ Take time to read God's Word and pray together as a family each day.

♦ Fill your home with music that honors Christ.

♦ Do not laugh at things that you have told your children are sinful.

♦ Teach your children that we are all personally accountable to Jesus Christ.

♦ Submit to the leadership of your husband, even if he is not all he should be.

♦ Love your wives and make this commitment, *"I will never leave thee, nor forsake thee."*

♦ Do not provoke your children to wrath by hypocrisy, unrealistic expectations, or an unforgiving spirit.

*"And the L*ord *God said, It is not good that the man should be alone; I will make him an help meet for him . . . and the rib, which the L*ord *God had taken from man, made he a woman, and brought her unto the man. And Adam said, This is now bone of my bones, and flesh of my flesh: she shall be called Woman, because she was taken out of Man. Therefore shall a man leave his father and his mother, and shall cleave unto his wife: and they shall be one flesh."*

Genesis 2:18, 22-24

Chapter Two

Marriage by Divine Design

 od united the first man and woman in holy matrimony, establishing the institution of marriage. We visit the scene of the first marriage ceremony in Genesis chapter two.

The Bible says in Genesis 2:18-24,

And the LORD God said, It is not good that the man should be alone; I will make him an help meet for him. And out of the ground the LORD God formed every beast of the field, and every fowl of the air; and brought them unto Adam to see what he would call them: and whatsoever Adam called every living creature, that was the name thereof. And Adam gave names to all cattle, and to the fowl of the air, and to every beast of the

field; but for Adam there was not found an help meet for him. And the LORD God caused a deep sleep to fall upon Adam, and he slept: and he took one of his ribs, and closed up the flesh instead thereof; and the rib, which the LORD God had taken from man, made he a woman, and brought her unto the man. And Adam said, This is now bone of my bones, and flesh of my flesh: she shall be called Woman, because she was taken out of Man. Therefore shall a man leave his father and his mother, and shall cleave unto his wife: and they shall be one flesh.

Here we find marriage by divine design. There is no other way we should view marriage except the way God gives it to us–by divine design.

> *The key to finding the person God wants you to marry is to go to sleep in God's will, to rest completely in Jesus Christ and allow His will to be done.*

Follow the Scriptures in your marriage. The Bible takes us right back to Genesis chapter two with Adam and Eve in the Garden of Eden. First there was Adam, without Eve. God saw that it was *"not good that the man should be alone"* (Genesis 2:18). What did He do? He caused a deep sleep to come upon Adam. He took a rib from Adam, and from that rib He created a woman. Adam awoke and saw the most beautiful creature he had ever looked upon. Not only was she gorgeous, no doubt the most gorgeous woman who ever lived, but she was the perfect person God created for Adam. She was his absolute completer. Adam and Eve were a perfect match.

How did Adam get that wife? Though the Bible does not tell us specifically, it would have been an immoral thing for God to force Adam to sleep against his own will. No doubt Adam submitted to God's decision to put him to sleep. He gave absolute trust to the Lord. He may have said, "Lord, I'm taking my hands off this completely. I'm not going to look for a mate. I'm not searching for a wife. I'm going to sleep in the will of God." He allowed God to bring the woman into his life that God chose for him.

The key to finding the person God wants you to marry is to go to sleep in God's will, to rest completely in Jesus Christ and allow His will to be done. Perhaps this is the only thing keeping some of you from getting married. It is not that the person is not available. It is that you are not available to God as you should be so that God can bring that person into your life. Sleep in the will of God and allow God to bring to you the person of His choosing.

Recently, I heard a survey about failures among families. One group said, "I have failed in the matter of controlling my weight." Another group said, "I am far too much in debt; I have failed in family finances."

The one thing not mentioned in that particular survey was that over one half of all marriages end in divorce. The most troubling thing about this statistic is that there are almost as many church-going couples whose marriages fail as there are non-church-going couples whose marriages fail. May God help those of us who know the Lord as our Savior to do what we should concerning the matter of marriage.

We are given the foundation for marriage in the first chapter of Genesis. The Bible says in verse twenty-eight, *"And God blessed them, and God said unto them, Be fruitful, and multiply, and replenish the earth, and subdue it: and have dominion over the fish of the sea, and over the fowl of the air, and over every living thing that moveth upon the earth."*

When we read the Bible casually, it is easy to miss God's intention and direction. The Bible says the responsibility of the first couple was to be fruitful and multiply, to replenish the earth. This is God's way. He has designed men and women so that they might fulfill this commandment.

If you want to change not only a country, but an entire civilization, then change the way they perceive the idea of sexuality. The foundation for the continuation of the civilized world, as God has intended for it to be, is rooted in this statement, "The cornerstone is the Christian home, the home built on Jesus Christ. The cornerstone is the family unit–the husband and wife."

What does it mean to have the family and marriage redefined? According to the enemies of the Bible, we are in a crisis which has been created by the "patriarchal" society, meaning, our "men-led world." It is their goal to destroy the patriarchal society and reconstruct a society that is lived according to their beliefs and values. Christians need to keep in mind that the patriarchal society is not a Western idea, it is a biblical truth. Men are to lead their families.

Over seventy percent of the American population believes that we are in a moral values crisis. At the same time, over seventy percent of the American population believes there are no absolutes. There is no group of moral values on which we will all agree. If they are saying that our crisis is one of moral values, and at the same time they cannot agree on what is morally right, then it is absolutely impossible to change the moral downslide of our nation.

Where does this leave the Christian? Where does this leave the family that wants to rear children to grow up with beliefs and values rooted in the Word of God? Where does this leave those of us who believe that God has a divine design for marriage? It leaves us with no options. We must go back to the Garden of

Eden and take God's Word as it is. As Bible-believing Christians, we must practice nothing but what we find in the Scriptures.

To have marriage by divine design, we must remember some things. Make note of the following Bible verses so when your children ask you questions, you will be able to answer them. The answers need to be more than your opinion. Children are going to be bombarded with what they have been told is the majority opinion, and it will differ from your opinion. We must firmly fix in their minds that the Bible is the inerrant Word of God, that it is God's Word for all time, and that God's children, with God's help, must seek to adhere to the standards of God's Word.

> *The husband is a child of his parents; but when he takes on the responsibility of marriage, he is to have the authority of his own home.*

THE PATTERN FOR MARRIAGE

If we are going to have marriage by divine design, which is the foundation of all civilization, then we must see that God has designed a pattern for marriage. He has made it simple to find and follow that pattern.

In Genesis 2:21-24 the Bible says,

> *And the LORD God caused a deep sleep to fall upon Adam, and he slept: and he took one of his ribs, and closed up the flesh instead thereof; and the rib, which the LORD God had taken from man, made he a woman, and brought her unto the man.*

> *And Adam said, This is now bone of my bones, and flesh of my flesh: she shall be called Woman, because she was taken out of Man. Therefore shall a man leave his father and his mother, and shall cleave unto his wife: and they shall be one flesh.*

Once I accepted Genesis 1:1, *"In the beginning God created the heaven and the earth,"* I have not had trouble with anything else in the Bible. It is all God's Word; it is all true.

God created Adam from the dust of the earth. He took a rib out of Adam's side and created Eve to be his wife. The Bible says that a man is to leave his father and mother. We all know that Adam and Eve had no earthly parents, yet in the pattern God gave, a man is to leave his father and mother. The husband is a child of his parents; but when he takes on the responsibility of marriage, he is to have the authority of his own home. He is no longer to be treated as a child by his parents.

This does not mean that he must leave town. In some instances, he may live in the same dwelling as his parents; though that can become difficult. It means that he does not depend upon his parents as a child would depend upon his mother and father. He must leave his mother and father and cleave unto his wife. Without this leaving, there cannot be the cleaving that brings oneness in marriage.

In Genesis 5:1-5 the Bible says,

> *This is the book of the generations of Adam. In the day that God created man, in the likeness of God made he him; male and female created he them; and blessed them, and called their name Adam, in the day when they were created. And Adam lived an hundred and thirty years, and begat a son in his own likeness, after his image; and called his name Seth: and the days of Adam*

after he had begotten Seth were eight hundred years: and he begat sons and daughters: and all the days that Adam lived were nine hundred and thirty years: and he died.

Notice that verse two says, *"Male and female created he them."* This is God's pattern. A man is to marry a woman; a woman is to marry a man. A man is not to marry a man, and a woman is not to marry a woman. If we are going to have marriage according to God's design, we must follow the pattern God has given.

Did you ever imagine that you would have to deal with the issues that we face today? Did you ever imagine that in our world we would have to try to explain such things to children? We find early in Scripture that people had to deal with these same problems centuries ago, and God gave them answers. The answers He gave to them are the same answers that we need in this perplexing generation in which we live.

The Bible says in Leviticus 18:22, *"Thou shalt not lie with mankind, as with womankind: it is abomination."* This does not mean that a man cannot lie down and rest if there is another man resting near him. This verse has to do with a sexual relationship. The Bible says that a man should not have a sexual relationship with another man, and a woman should not have that relationship with another woman. This is plainly taught in God's Word. The Bible says this is an *"abomination."*

The word *"abomination"* is an interesting word. At times this word is used loosely around religious settings or churches, but it is a very powerful word. It has to do with the subject of sin; and not just any sin, but the most hideous of all sins being practiced in any civilization. God says that not only is this sinful, it is at the lowest rung of sinful behavior. It is an *"abomination."* It is not something to be promoted or applauded.

The thing that should convict us is not the matter of whether or not we are going to practice this sin, but that we, as Christians, should set such wonderful examples in our own marriages that young people would desire the same. We should pray, "Lord, help me to live in such a way before young people and all people that they will see the Christian marriage we have and will desire to have this kind of relationship in their lives." We should strive to be exemplary in our marriages as Christians. Marriage by divine design is according to the pattern God has set in His Word. We represent the wonderful relationship that Christ, our heavenly Groom, has with His bride, the church.

You may think, "I have my children in a Christian school. I have a Christian home. That is all they need." If you feel this way, you have failed to realize we are in a war. Do not be so naive as to think your children are not going to come into contact with other children who are growing up with a completely different value system than your children. Your children are going to be challenged about what they believe and what they have been taught.

> *Marriage by divine design is according to the pattern God has set in His Word.*

You may be thinking, "If I just teach what is true, that will be enough. If I just bombard them with verses from the Bible, if I send them to a Christian school, that will be enough. If I get them in Sunday School, that will be enough." This will not be enough. If they do not see a Christian marriage lived in your home, no amount of Sunday School, no amount of Christian school, and no amount of church attendance will be enough. May God help us to have a marriage that is truly by divine design.

THE PURITY IN MARRIAGE

The Bible says in the New Testament book of Hebrews, chapter thirteen, verses one through four,

> *Let brotherly love continue. Be not forgetful to entertain strangers: for thereby some have entertained angels unawares. Remember them that are in bonds, as bound with them; and them which suffer adversity, as being yourselves also in the body. Marriage is honourable in all, and the bed undefiled: but whoremongers and adulterers God will judge.*

Our marriages are to be pure. We are to say, "Lord, I will be the husband that this woman deserves to have," or "Lord, I will be the wife this man deserves to have." When we get married, we make a covenant with God and with one another. We are held accountable before God to be faithful to our husbands or wives and not to break our marriage covenant by having an impure relationship with another person.

There are two words to make special note of used in Hebrews chapter thirteen, *"whoremongers"* and *"adulterers."* These are not pretty words. These are strong, powerful words.

Your children are going to be challenged about what they believe and what they have been taught.

I once read part of the early laws written for the state of Connecticut about how adulterers and adulteresses were dealt with and judged. In their definition, if a married man engaged in sexual activity with an unmarried woman, he was considered an adulterer; she was known as a fornicator or a practitioner of lewd, sexual behavior. If a married woman engaged in sexual behavior with an unmarried man, she was considered to be an adulteress, and the unmarried man was considered to have engaged in lewd, sexual behavior. If both parties were married and engaged in sexual behavior with someone they were not married to, they were both considered adulterers. In other words, the word *adulterer* was correctly dealt with by the state of Connecticut years ago. In its biblical context, an adulterer is someone in a marriage union who breaks that relationship of purity by engaging in sexual activity with another person.

The Bible also uses the word *"whoremongers."* The Word of God clearly teaches that we are not to engage in the sexual relationship until marriage, and then only with the one to whom we are married. We need to lift up our voices and declare this truth without apology.

> *We should be faithful in the marriage relationship because God says it is His design.*

People are talking much today about disease. It is shocking to hear of how many teenagers already have an incurable sexually-transmitted disease. Perhaps as many as one out of two hundred seventy Americans already has the HIV virus.

If you say, "I am not going to engage in this kind of behavior. I am going to be faithful to my wife or faithful to my husband. I am going to be pure in my relationship because I am afraid of disease," you have the wrong motive.

We should be faithful in the marriage relationship because God says it is His design. We should fear God, love God, and be obedient to God; knowing that if we break our covenant relationship in marriage, God will judge us. The Bible says in

Hebrews 13:4, *"Marriage is honourable in all, and the bed undefiled: but whoremongers and adulterers God will judge."*

Notice what the Bible says in Proverbs 2:11-16,

> *Discretion shall preserve thee, understanding shall keep thee: to deliver thee from the way of the evil man, from the man that speaketh froward things; who leave the paths of uprightness, to walk in the ways of darkness; who rejoice to do evil, and delight in the frowardness of the wicked; whose ways are crooked, and they froward in their paths: to deliver thee from the strange woman...*

Let us seek to understand the idea of a *"strange woman."* This does not mean that she looks strange. It does not mean that she behaves in some strange fashion. For someone to be *"strange,"* in the sense of the Bible word, simply means that person does not belong to you.

My wife, when speaking to someone about me, refers to me as her husband. She considers that I belong to her; I am her husband. When I speak of her in my conversation to others I say, "She is my wife." By using the personal pronoun *my*, I am saying that she belongs to me; she is mine.

We belong to one another as we belong to God. No other woman is mine, and no other man is hers. Every other woman, in this sense, is a stranger to me. Every other man, in this sense, is a stranger to her.

When you are married, no woman other than your wife belongs to you. Wives, no man but your husband belongs to you. You should not begin to develop any interest in any other man or any other woman because that person does not belong to you.

Gentlemen, a woman may try to catch your eye; or ladies, a man may make some comment about how you look. Watch out! You are about to begin to engage in what could be the greatest tragedy of your life!

The Bible continues in verses sixteen through nineteen of Proverbs chapter two,

> *To deliver thee from the strange woman, even from the stranger which flattereth with her words; which forsaketh the guide of her youth, and forgetteth the covenant of her God. For her house inclineth unto death, and her paths unto the dead. None that go unto her return again, neither take they hold of the paths of life.*

Guard against this woman who *"flattereth with her words,"* *"forsaketh the guide of her youth,"* and *"forgetteth the covenant of her God."*

In Proverbs 6:24-26 the Bible says,

> *To keep thee from the evil woman, from the flattery of the tongue of a strange woman. Lust not after her beauty in thine heart; neither let her take thee with her eyelids. For by means of a whorish woman a man is brought to a piece of bread: and the adulteress will hunt for the precious life.*

What you may see in the beginning is a pleasant-looking person. It may be a person of means and ability. In the end, this relationship with someone who does not belong to you will bring you *"to a piece of bread."* Take God at His Word. Marriage according to divine design has purity.

THE PERMANENCY OF MARRIAGE

Marriage by divine design has permanency. There are many people I deal with who are married for their second or third time. In my own life and ministry, I would never mistreat someone no matter how many times he or she has been married. Many of these people work and serve God so wonderfully and beautifully that I do not know what I would do without them. They are getting on with their lives, and I praise the Lord for them.

If you have had the unfortunate experience of going through a failure in marriage, I am sure you have come to realize that unless you get some things established in your life that are biblical and true, you are apt to repeat the same failure. We need to hear the truth.

The Bible says in Matthew 19:3-9,

> *The Pharisees also came unto him, tempting him, and saying unto him, Is it lawful for a man to put away his wife for every cause? And he answered and said unto them, Have ye not read, that he which made them at the beginning made them male and female, and said, For this cause shall a man leave father and mother, and shall cleave to his wife: and they twain shall be one flesh? Wherefore they are no more twain, but one flesh. What therefore God hath joined together, let not man put asunder. They say unto him, Why did Moses then command to give a writing of divorcement, and to put her away? He saith unto them, Moses because of the hardness of your hearts suffered you to put away your wives: but from the beginning it was not so. And I say unto you, Whosoever shall put away his wife, except it be for fornication, and shall marry another,*

*committeth adultery: and whoso marrieth her
which is put away doth commit adultery.*

Unless we are willing to take all that the Bible says about the subject of marriage and put it together, we are going to get a one-sided view. I personally do not believe that the argument about marriage and divorce will ever be settled to the satisfaction of all God's children, but I want no confusion about this point—the Lord Jesus Christ, from the beginning, said emphatically that it was God's design for a marriage to be permanent. When He was asked about Moses giving a bill of divorcement, the Lord Jesus answered, *"But from the beginning it was not so."* It is God's original, divine design that marriage be permanent.

> *Unless we are willing to take all that the Bible says about the subject of marriage and put it together, we are going to get a one-sided view.*

If you have been married, divorced, and remarried; then I say to you, God bless you. Determine that you are going to live the rest of your life with your mate and put the principles of God's Word to work in your marriage.

Homes and families are hurting. We are living in a wicked society where many do what is right in their own eyes and justify their actions fully. Ideas so contrary to the Bible have become institutionalized in the thinking of people. This is why it is much more important for those of us who claim to be Bible-believing Christians to tell the truth in love and not try to accommodate the decaying morals and behavior of our present world.

May God help us to have marriages by divine design.

Home Work

♦ Know the pattern for marriage taught in God's Word.

♦ Take the responsibility to teach your children what the Bible says about marriage.

♦ Be faithful to your mate and maintain purity in your marriage.

♦ Determine that you are going to stay with your spouse the rest of your life and put the principles of God's Word to work in your marriage.

"Rejoice evermore. Pray without ceasing. In every thing give thanks: for this is the will of God in Christ Jesus concerning you. Quench not the Spirit. Despise not prophesyings. Prove all things; hold fast that which is good. Abstain from all appearance of evil. And the very God of peace sanctify you wholly; and I pray God your whole spirit and soul and body be preserved blameless unto the coming of our Lord Jesus Christ."

I Thessalonians 5:16-23

Chapter Three

Establish a Spiritual Foundation in Marriage

 hristians, in the bond of marriage, have been given the opportunity to represent the wonderful union that exists between Christ and His church.

The Bible says God has made us spirit, soul, and body. We are not simply a body, but *"spirit and soul and body."* When people use this phrase, they often begin with the body. But, there is a divine order we should always follow. The divine order is first spirit, then soul, and then body. In marriage, we are to be one in spirit, one in soul, and one in body.

From what we find in the earliest record of marriage in the Garden of Eden, we know that God told Adam to leave his father and mother, establishing a principle of leaving and cleaving. The Bible says in Genesis 2:24, *"Therefore shall a*

man leave his father and his mother, and shall cleave unto his wife: and they shall be one flesh."

There is a difference between unity and union. A husband and wife may agree on where they are to live. They may agree on what kind of car to drive. They may have a degree of *unity* in their marriage without having a *union*.

> From what we find in the earliest record of marriage in the Garden of Eden, we know that God told Adam to leave his father and mother, establishing a principle of leaving and cleaving.

It is amazing that many people contemplate marriage yet give no consideration to spiritual things. When asked, "What about your Christian life?" they often respond by saying, "We haven't talked about that." The foundation of marriage must be built on the Lord and our union in Christ.

I remember talking to a lady about her husband. She had been married about ten years, and she and her husband were having problems in their marriage. I said, "Is he a Christian?" She said, "I have no way of knowing." I said, "You've never asked him? You've never talked about it?" She said, "No, we just don't talk about those things. I don't know if he is a Christian or not." After hearing this, I did not wonder why she was having problems in her marriage.

God's Word says that we should not be unequally yoked together. Christian people should marry Christian people. However, some Christians are married to other Christians and are also unequally yoked because one is a Christian who loves the Lord and the other does not love the Lord.

Most people think that when they seek to become one in marriage, they become one in body. But no strong marriage can be built on oneness in body. If you are simply attracted to the physical, your marriage will not endure tough times. You may have found some *unity*, but there can be no real lasting *union*.

We are not just to have oneness in body but oneness in spirit, soul, and body. The spiritual union that we have with God and with one another lays the foundation for everything else in marriage.

What will help us to have this union? What will build the stability you must have if your home is to endure? If you are going to have the marriage God desires for you to have and enjoy the journey, you must establish a spiritual union.

SPEAK TO ONE ANOTHER ABOUT HOW YOU CAME TO KNOW THE LORD AND WHAT HE MEANS TO YOU

"Let the redeemed of the LORD say so, whom he hath redeemed from the hand of the enemy." Psalm 107:2

Men, your wife should be able to give your testimony as well as you could. She should know all there is to know about when you got saved and what Jesus Christ means to you. The reverse is also true. A husband should have heard his wife's testimony so often and heard her talk so much about the Lord Jesus that he is very familiar with how she came to know Jesus Christ as her Savior.

Can you give the details, not of your salvation, but of your mate's salvation? Have you talked together about how you came to know the Lord Jesus as your Savior and what He means to you?

When Evelyn and I were first married, we learned to speak often about knowing the Lord and about the wonderful blessings of God in our lives.

So many Christian people have been married for years and have never talked freely and openly about how they came to know the Lord as their Savior and what the Lord Jesus means to them. Establishing a spiritual union in marriage begins with speaking freely with your spouse about salvation and the blessings of God.

PRAY TOGETHER AND SHARE ANSWERS TO PRAYER

"Can two walk together, except they be agreed?" Amos 3:3

You will never know the heart of your spouse until you hear that person pray.

> *You will never know the heart of your spouse until you hear that person pray.*

When I hear my wife pray, there is something so precious about hearing her call my name and the names of my children in prayer and hearing her pray for the ministry God has given us. When I hear her call people's names out to God, when I hear her voice lifted to heaven, as we pray together, as we meet God on the common ground of prayer, I understand more about what the Bible says about dwelling with her according to knowledge. Husbands and wives should seek the Lord together in prayer and rejoice together in answered prayers.

READ GOD'S WORD TOGETHER AND SHARE WITH YOUR SPOUSE THE THINGS GOD HAS USED TO SPEAK TO YOU

"Thy word is a lamp unto my feet, and a light unto my path." Psalm 119:105

Perhaps you are not a good reader, and you are embarrassed to read in front of someone else. Do not allow that to be a stumbling block that causes you to neglect the Bible.

I enjoy hearing my wife read the Bible. I believe she enjoys hearing me read the Bible. We love to talk about the things in God's Word that He uses to speak to us.

You may say, "We never do that." Then eliminate some lesser things and begin to read the Bible together.

GIVE PRAYER REQUESTS TO ONE ANOTHER

"Bear ye one another's burdens, and so fulfil the law of Christ." Galatians 6:2

Pray about everything. When you are trying to make a decision, pray about it. When you deal with your children, pray that God will give you wisdom to deal with them together as parents.

It is hard to wait in marriage. It is hard to wait to purchase something we want, maybe a home or a car. But there is good instruction in the Bible that teaches us that we should make everything a matter of prayer. Let us ask God to help us pray about everything.

ATTEND CHURCH TOGETHER

"Not forsaking the assembling of ourselves together, as the manner of some is; but exhorting one another: and so much the more, as ye see the day approaching." Hebrews 10:25

Attend church together and talk about the blessings you have received as you worship God together. It would help so many of us when we leave the worship service not to talk about what went wrong or who was not there. We should talk about how God spoke to us and how the Holy Spirit penetrated our hearts.

SPEND TIME EACH DAY TALKING ABOUT GOD'S CARE OF YOUR LIVES

"Casting all your care upon him; for he careth for you." I Peter 5:7

Spend some uninterrupted time each day talking about God's grace and goodness in your lives. It will greatly benefit your marriage.

Every time my wife looks at me in our home, I have a book. I have books everywhere. Next to my chair there are books. In my bedroom there are books. In the drawers of the nightstands there are books. But there comes a time to stop everything and give attention to one another. Talk about how good God is and how God has cared for you during the day.

CHOOSE TO FORGIVE

"And be ye kind one to another, tenderhearted, forgiving one another, even as God for Christ's sake hath forgiven you." Ephesians 4:32

Decide when you get married that you are going to forgive one another. Make forgiveness a part of your life. Marriage must be a forgiving relationship.

> *Make forgiveness a part of your life. Marriage must be a forgiving relationship.*

We are to forgive because Christ has forgiven us. There is nothing for which God has not forgiven the believer. Our sins are washed away in the precious blood of Jesus Christ. Choose to forgive in your marriage as Christ has forgiven you.

BE WILLING TO ACCEPT REPROOF AND CORRECTION FROM ONE ANOTHER

"Faithful are the wounds of a friend; but the kisses of an enemy are deceitful." Proverbs 27:6

This is difficult to do. It is important to choose the right time and the right place for correction. Reproof should not be given in a public place or in front of other people. A spiritually mature man, secure in the love of his wife, will listen when she says, "For you to be the Christian you should be, this is something you need to correct."

A man should also be able to give reproof and correction to his wife when it is necessary. You can tell much about your spiritual maturity by the way you respond to loving reproof. Be willing to accept correction. It will help your marriage to grow.

SEEK CHRIST FOR VICTORY OVER ANNOYING HABITS IN YOUR LIFE

"For whatsoever is born of God overcometh the world: and this is the victory that overcometh the world, even our faith." I John 5:4

> *You can tell much about your spiritual maturity by the way you respond to loving reproof.*

Men like to say, "That's just the way I am. I lose my temper like that. You know I'm going to say something to the kids or say something to you I shouldn't say." Ask God to give you victory. You may never be perfect in the matter, but you can have victory over those habits. If you have a habit you know that you should not have, ask God to give you the victory. Every victory is won by daily abiding in the presence of the Lord.

Wives, if you pout and hold grudges, allowing the sun to go down on your wrath, that is not Christlike. Ask God to give you the victory.

ALLOW NOTHING UNCLEAN THROUGH YOUR EYE GATE

"I will set no wicked thing before mine eyes: I hate the work of them that turn aside; it shall not cleave to me." Psalm 101:3

With all the filth on television today, it is difficult not to look at vile things. But when we allow unclean things into our minds, we sin against our marriage. When we allow our intellect to be motivated and our emotions to be stirred by some wicked thing that violates our marriage, when our will is given over to sin in our thought life, we have disrupted the spiritual union God desires for us to have.

Not only men, but also women can get involved in these same kinds of things. Watch your eye gate. If you want this spiritual union, do not let evil things into your eye gate.

DESIRE THE SPIRIT OF CHRIST IN YOUR MARRIED LIFE

"Let this mind be in you, which was also in Christ Jesus."
Philippians 2:5

So many believers are content to call themselves Christians and yet do not desire to be like Christ. Put yourself to the test. For example, consider the tone of your voice. I can be a demanding, authoritative kind of person. The tone of my voice can be harsh, hard, driving, and distant. It is something in which I greatly need God's help. This is not something that is accomplished from trying; it is something you get from dying–dying to self.

When children come along, the husband and wife need to be together, not just under the same roof, but together in spirit to deal with the problems and difficulties their children will have. If you think when your children are grown and gone you have finished helping them, you are wrong. Ask someone who has grown children. They still need counsel from a spiritual mother and father.

It saddens me to think of how many people have settled into simply having "a marriage" and have not allowed God to really do for them what He desires to do. Desire the spirit of Christ in your marriage.

To have been with the Lord Jesus would have been wonderful. If you will live for Jesus Christ and truly give yourself to Him, your mate will have someone he or she can live with who is like the Lord Jesus.

BUILD YOUR LIFE AROUND THE LORD

"And he is the head of the body, the church: who is the beginning, the firstborn from the dead; that in all things he might have the preeminence." Colossians 1:18

Build your life around the Lord, not your children, not activities, and not hobbies. Many people have built their married life around their children. When their children are gone, they have no married life left. They really did not have one in the first place.

> *It saddens me to think of how many people have settled into simply having "a marriage" and have not allowed God to really do for them what He desires to do.*

I love being with my wife, and she loves being with me. She can calm my troubled heart. We have a spiritual common ground on which we can stand. May God help that to endure to our dying day.

I am devoted to my children. I want to be a good grandparent to my grandchildren. But my life cannot be built around my wife, my children or my grandchildren; it must be built around the Lord Jesus. As my wife and I love the Lord, we grow to love one another more. Imagine our relationship as a triangle. The Lord is at the peak, she is at one corner, and I am at the other corner. As we both move up closer to God, we move closer to one another. Build your married life around the Lord Jesus.

EXALT CHRIST TO ONE ANOTHER

"O magnify the LORD *with me, and let us exalt his name together."* Psalm 34:3

In your home, praise the Lord and speak of the goodness of God. Magnify the Lord Jesus and develop an attitude in your conversation that exalts Christ. There is a sweet, precious fragrance to marriage when Christ is lifted up. It helps to lighten the everyday burdens. Talk about how wonderful the Lord is to you and your family.

CULTIVATE A SPIRIT OF GRATITUDE

"And let the peace of God rule in your hearts, to the which also ye are called in one body; and be ye thankful." Colossians 3:15

So much is said about gratitude in the Bible. Ephesians 5:28-29 says, *"So ought men to love their wives as their own bodies. He that loveth his wife loveth himself. For no man ever yet hated his own flesh; but nourisheth and cherisheth it, even as the Lord the church."*

> *There is a sweet, precious fragrance to marriage when Christ is lifted up.*

If we are not careful, we form a habit of griping and complaining. We have a habit of finding the worst and not seeing the best, of being critical and not praising. We think we are straightening everything out by talking about everything that is wrong.

Let me give you some suggestions to help you cultivate a spirit of gratitude. Visit a nursing home. Go into the rooms and speak to people who never have anyone to touch them or hug them or take their hand and love them, who never have anyone sit down and talk to them for a period of time. The people who are there, in some cases, have gone into a world of loneliness never to come out until they leave this world. This will make you grateful.

Visit a hospital, especially a pediatric hospital. Walk into a room where parents are waiting while their children's lives are hanging in the balance. They do not know if their little babies are going to make it through the night. Visit a place like that and you will have a deeper appreciation for what God has done in giving your children health.

Go to a funeral home. See a grieving family and be thankful to God that you have life and strength and that you still have an opportunity to live for Him. As long as there is life, there is hope to make things right.

Witness to people who are without Christ and see how terrible it is to be without God and without hope in this world, headed toward hell and destruction. To have a spiritual marriage, we must cultivate a spirit of gratitude.

TAKE YOUR RIGHTFUL PLACE IN MARRIAGE

"Submitting yourselves one to another in the fear of God."
Ephesians 5:21

The Bible says a woman should reverence her husband. So many men live in a way that makes it difficult for their wives to reverence them. Every Christian woman should have the privilege of being married to a truly spiritual man who has the tenderness of Jesus Christ, a man who can feel, touch, love, and care.

Ephesians 5:22 says, *"Wives, submit yourselves unto your own husbands, as unto the Lord."* This is the wife's place.

Verse twenty-five says, *"Husbands, love your wives, even as Christ also loved the church, and gave himself for it."* We certainly cannot love our wives to the degree that Christ loves us, but we can love them in the same way.

Husband, your place is to lead. Wife, your place is to submit. Submission does not mean silence, but it does mean knowing when and where to speak. This is especially true in the matter of a wife correcting her husband. Do you know where we find the ability to lead and the ability to submit? We find this ability in spiritual union with Christ.

A man leads in this spiritual union. He loves the Lord. He may not be eloquent, handsome, or even financially secure, but his wife admires how he loves God. She knows that he meets the Lord Jesus and finds what God wants his family to do. She honors, reverences, and respects him because he is a man of God and a spiritual leader.

Gentlemen, be a spiritual leader who loves Jesus Christ. Your wife will love and admire the way you love Christ. Wife, your place is to submit to the authority of your husband's leadership in your home. You cannot honor God and obey God without being submissive to your husband.

You may say, "I know more than he knows." Most women do know more than their husbands know. You say, "I can do a lot of things he can't do." Most women can do more things than their husbands can do. But as a Christian, you are to yield to your husband's leadership in your life. Maybe you are a strong-willed person. Maybe you were taught to express yourself that way.

But your place, according to God's Word, is in submission to your husband.

I am praying that people will learn what it means to establish a spiritual relationship in marriage, to be one in Christ, to be joined together in spirit, soul, and body. I am praying that people will have the blessed privilege of journeying to glory in marital union with a mate who loves the Lord Jesus and is looking for His return. How good God is to all of us to allow us to know from the Bible these things that will help us to have a spiritual union in marriage.

Home Work

♦ Speak to one another about how you came to know Christ and what He means to you.

♦ Pray together and share answers to prayer.

♦ Read God's Word together and share the things God has used to speak to you.

♦ Give prayer requests to one another.

♦ Attend church together and talk about the blessings you received from the service.

♦ Spend time each day talking about God's care of your lives.

♦ Choose to forgive one another as Christ has forgiven you.

♦ Be willing to accept reproof and choose the right time to give reproof to one another.

♦ Seek Christ for victory over annoying habits in your life.

♦ Allow nothing unclean to come through your eye gate.

♦ Desire the spirit of Christ in your married life.

♦ Build your life around the Lord, not your children, activities, or hobbies.

♦ Exalt Christ in the home by praising Him and speaking of His goodness.

♦ Cultivate a spirit of gratitude.

♦ Take your rightful place in marriage.

*"Husbands, love your wives, even
as Christ also loved the church, and
gave himself for it."*

Ephesians 5:25

Chapter Four

Calvary Love in the Christian Home

he first time I ever saw the girl who would become my wife, we were in our high school auditorium for study hall. We could sit anywhere we pleased; at least most of the students could. I had been asked to sit on the front row, right in front of the teacher. Two of my friends were seated next to me.

I turned around and saw a girl standing in the back of the auditorium. She had on a lovely white dress. She had a dark complexion, dark hair, and dark eyes. I elbowed the guy next to me and said, "Don't look now, but there is an angel standing in the back. She's the prettiest thing I've ever seen in my life."

He turned around and saw who it was and said, "Get her off your mind, man. Her brother is a terror. If you even think about her and he finds out about it, he will tear your arms off."

57

The truth of the matter is, that same boy lived across the road from the girl standing in the back, and he was madly in love with her. She cared nothing for him, but he told all the boys that crazy story to keep them away from her. It did not work. I have been married to her since 1967.

The first time she and I were ever together to have what some people might call a date, it snowed. We walked through a field in the snow. I still remember the snowflakes falling on her beautiful face. I turned again and again to look at her. Even now I think of that day every time it snows.

I was sitting recently on a park bench on our Crown College campus talking to one of the men who teaches for us. He is seventy-six years old. He said to me, "You really love your wife and everybody knows it. I've been married for half a century, and I want to tell you a little secret–you will love her more and more. In just a few minutes, I am going to take my wife to lunch. I am as excited as a school boy on a first date." I said, "Thank you. That encourages me."

The Word of God says in Ephesians 5:25, *"Husbands, love your wives, even as Christ also loved the church, and gave himself for it."*

The strongest love ever known is "Calvary love." Let us have this "Calvary love" in our Christian homes. Just because you are a Christian does not mean you have a Christian marriage. Just because you are a Christian does not mean you have a Christian home. There are many people who assume that if two Christians marry, they have a Christian home. It does not work that way.

The Christian marriage and the Christian home have much more to do with what we put into them than what we take out of them. Some folks have what could be called "Christian house cleaning." They get everything out that they think is improper, but they do not put the right things into their homes. They still do not have a Christian home or a Christian marriage.

The beautiful relationship we have with our wives is to be a lovely type of the relationship Jesus Christ has with His church. We are to reflect that relationship. This is why we should give the more earnest heed to our marriages. The world needs to see Christ in our homes. Our marriages also reflect the testimony of our church. If our marriages are not what they should be, then our church does not have the testimony it should have. This is a serious matter. We have the glorious privilege of, not only representing our Lord, but also representing the testimony of our church by the home and marriage we have. May God help us in this matter.

> *The beautiful relationship we have with our wives is to be a lovely type of the relationship Jesus Christ has with His church. We are to reflect that relationship.*

The Bible says, *"Husbands, love your wives, even as Christ also loved the church, and gave himself for it."* This is Calvary love. The Lord Jesus loved the church and gave Himself for it.

There are passages in the Bible that deal with women, wives and mothers. There are passages in the Bible that deal with fathers and what fathers should do and should not do. There are passages in the Bible that deal with the responsibilities and the joys of being a grandparent. There are many passages in the Bible that deal with the responsibilities of children and their accountability to God.

In this passage, God targets husbands. Perhaps you are not a husband, but you desire to have Calvary love in your home.

I am appalled at the instruction for the home that so many Christians are willing to accept. So much of so-called "family instruction" is not Christian instruction. Let us imagine that someone travels all over the country having family counseling sessions. He goes to a place and talks to people who are not Christians. He says, "Here are certain principles. Here are some things that will help you with intimacy. Here are some things that will help you be polite and kind." All the things he shares with people are good ideas. Then he goes to the next group carrying his books and all his tapes and says, "I am going to have a marriage counseling session here." This group happens to be a church group. He gives the same information to the people in the church who claim to be Christians that he gives to people who are not Christians. Christians are indwelt by the Holy Spirit. They have a resource that those who are not Christians do not have. Is there no difference in being a child of God and not being a child of God? Is there no difference in the ability God gives us, as His children, to have the right kind of marriage and the ability of those who are not children of God to deal with the struggles people go through in trying to have a marriage? Is there no difference in being a Christian and not being a Christian? Certainly there is.

In the fifth chapter of Romans, the Bible says in verses one through five,

> *Therefore being justified by faith, we have peace with God through our Lord Jesus Christ: By whom also we have access by faith into this grace wherein we stand, and rejoice in hope of the glory of God. And not only so, but we glory in tribulations also: knowing that tribulation worketh patience; And patience, experience; and experience, hope: And hope maketh not ashamed; because the love of God is shed abroad in our hearts by the Holy Ghost which is given unto us.*

What does this mean? Certainly it means that God loves us, but it also means that God gives us the capacity as Christians to love people with the love of God. This is a work done through us by the Holy Spirit of God. People who are not saved are not capable of this because they have not been born of the Spirit of God.

I know many people who are married, but not happily married. Many married couples in the ministry are not happily married. Many in the church who are married are not happily married. The way to correct what is wrong in the Christian life is to go straight to the heart of the matter, which is the spiritual condition. This is the foundation for it all.

The Bible targets the husband and says the husband is to love his wife with a Calvary love, to love her as Christ loved the church and gave Himself for it. This is Calvary love in the Christian home.

CALVARY LOVE IS A COVENANT LOVE

In the fifth chapter of Proverbs we find a solemn warning. The Bible says in verses one through three,

> *My son, attend unto my wisdom, and bow*
> *thine ear to my understanding: that thou mayest*
> *regard discretion, and that thy lips may keep*
> *knowledge. For the lips of a strange woman...*

The word *"strange"* in this passage means one who does not belong to you. She is not yours to touch. This does not mean she looks strange. The strange woman is a woman who does not belong to you.

The Bible continues in verse three, *"For the lips of a strange woman drop as an honeycomb, and her mouth is smoother than oil."* We wonder why some fellow runs off with the ugliest girl in town. It has nothing to do with looks; it has everything to do with strange flesh.

The Bible says in verses four and five, *"But her end is bitter as wormwood, sharp as a twoedged sword. Her feet go down to death; her steps take hold on hell."* Do not look at her lips. Do not look at her eyes. Look at her feet! They are planted in hell.

Verse six says, *"Lest thou shouldest ponder the path of life, her ways are moveable, that thou canst not know them."* She will dart in and out of your mind.

> *Hear me now therefore, O ye children, and depart not from the words of my mouth. Remove thy way far from her, and come not nigh the door of her house: lest thou give thine honour unto others, and thy years unto the cruel: lest strangers be filled with thy wealth; and thy labours be in the house of a stranger; and thou mourn at the last, when thy flesh and thy body are consumed, and say, How have I hated instruction, and my heart despised reproof; and have not obeyed the voice of my teachers, nor inclined mine ear to them that instructed me!* (Proverbs 5:7-13)

The Word of God says in Proverbs 5:18, *"Let thy fountain be blessed: and rejoice with the wife of thy youth."* Our old nature is not like someone getting trapped in quick sand. The old nature is not like a child walking through the woods and falling into a pit. The old nature is like a wild beast—hungry, thirsty, longing for something to eat, searching it out, pacing back and forth trying to find something on which to feed.

You will change your life and your schedule just to walk by and catch a glimpse. Your life will begin to revolve around your desire for strange flesh. Your mind will race with ideas of what you should not do. You may have felt the touch of her hand, but look at her feet. Her steps take hold on hell! Proverbs 6:26 says, *"For by means of a whorish woman a man is brought to a piece of bread."* May God help us. When you think of following after a strange woman, think of who you are in Christ Jesus. Think of whom you represent to a lost and dying world. Think of the testimony of your church.

Calvary love is a covenant love. In Malachi 2:14 the Bible says, *"Yet ye say, Wherefore? Because the LORD hath been witness between thee and the wife of thy youth, against whom thou hast dealt treacherously: yet is she thy companion, and the wife of thy covenant."*

Marriage for a Christian is not a contract. When you make a contract to buy a car, someone says, "If you don't pay for this car, we'll repossess it." When you make a contract to buy a house, the lender says, "If you don't make the payment on time, you have just so many days of grace. After a while, we are going to come and evict you." When you make a contract to buy insurance, the agent says, "If you don't pay the premium, we'll cancel your coverage." Marriage is not a contract.

Marriage is a covenant. We do not make this covenant with one another, but with God. The man makes a covenant with God, "God, I covenant with Thee that I will be the husband to this wife that You desire for me to be and that she deserves to have." The woman makes a covenant with God, "Lord, I covenant with Thee, I promise Thee that I will be the faithful wife to this man that You desire for me to be and that he deserves to have."

Calvary love is a covenant love. In John chapter seventeen, when the Lord Jesus Christ prayed that great high priestly prayer, the Bible says in verses one through ten,

These words spake Jesus, and lifted up his eyes to heaven, and said, Father, the hour is come; glorify thy Son, that thy Son also may glorify thee: as thou hast given him power over all flesh, that he should give eternal life to as many as thou hast given him. And this is life eternal, that they might know thee the only true God, and Jesus Christ, whom thou hast sent. I have glorified thee on the earth: I have finished the work which thou gavest me to do. And now, O Father, glorify thou me with thine own self with the glory which I had with thee before the world was. I have manifested thy name unto the men which thou gavest me out of the world: thine they were, and thou gavest them me; and they have kept thy word. Now they have known that all things whatsoever thou hast given me are of thee. For I have given unto them the words which thou gavest me; and they have received them, and have known surely that I came out from thee, and they have believed that thou didst send me. I pray for them: I pray not for the world, but for them which thou hast given me; for they are thine. And all mine are thine, and thine are mine; and I am glorified in them.

We cannot read this prayer without hearing again and again, *"which thou gavest me," "which thou gavest me," "which thou gavest me."* When we hold the cup in our hands to observe the memorial supper that Christ left His church, we observe this ordinance in remembrance of Him. When we speak about this covenant, it is not a covenant with God the Father that we remember when we hold that cup and take that bread. It is the covenant that God has with His Son that all who come to God by faith in the Son the Father will give the Son. This is the covenant that God the Father has with God the Son. At salvation, we enter into a covenant relationship; the covenant is between God the Father and God the Son.

As we enter the relationship of marriage, God says we enter into a covenant relationship with Him. We covenant with God in a Calvary love. We covenant with God that we will be what God expects for us to be. Wives will change, and husbands will change, but God never changes. Let us keep this covenant with our God.

CALVARY LOVE IS A CAUSING LOVE

The Bible says in I John 4:19, *"We love him, because he first loved us."* Why do we love the Lord Jesus? We love Him because He first loved us. We have responded to His love. Jesus Christ has caused us to love Him.

This is where we, as bride and groom, represent the beautiful relationship that Christ has with His church. The Bible says, *"Husbands, love your wives, even as Christ also loved the church."* How does the church learn to love the Lord? He causes the church to love Him.

> *Marriage is a covenant. We do not make this covenant with one another, but with God.*

Husbands are to cause their wives to love them. I hear some men saying, "I'm not married to the sweetest woman in the world." I want to say to them, "When you married her, she was probably much sweeter than she is today. If she has been married to you for a while, she has probably had to get tough to live with you." Many men have made something out of their wives that they do not like. They have no one to blame but themselves. Early on they whispered, "Darling. Sweetheart. Dumpling." Today, if it is anything, it is, "Hey, you!" We can cause our wives to love us by the way we speak to them.

Our neighbors have a dog that is a Jack Russell terrier. I did not know the name of the animal when I first saw it, so I just called him Jack. You know how neighbors' dogs are; they are always into your things. I would find myself constantly saying, "Jack's out here again. Jack, what are you doing here? Jack, get off my porch. Jack, stop dragging my things everywhere." For some reason that little dog enjoyed being around me. I thought to myself, "All right, Jack, I'll touch your head. All right, Jack, I'll pet you. All right, Jack, I'll be nice to you. Come here, Jack. Come on, Jack. You want to sit beside me, Jack?" I said to my wife one day, "Jack is gaining weight." I found out that dog was not Jack after all. She was Jackie! Do you know what Jackie did? She made me love her by simply loving me. After a while, I could not tell her to go home. As a matter of fact, I started saying things like, "I wonder if they want to get rid of that dog. She would make a nice pet for my grandchildren." That crazy dog caused me to love her.

Gentlemen, we must work at causing our wives to love us. Every woman should have the privilege of being married to a man who looks after her better than she can look after herself. Is that not what you promised you would do when you married her? You may say, "Well, I didn't know I was marrying a military sergeant." Well, you married her, and you are married to the right woman.

If you say, "I love you, darling," she will say, "I love you, too, sweetie." Do you know why? Because God made her to answer back to you. If you yell at her, she will yell back at you. If you whisper to her, she will whisper to you. We must work at it. We get under all kinds of pressure. Every day is an emergency.

Whatever the immediate happens to be, it appears overwhelming. The people you love the most in life, at least the ones you say you love the most in life, hear you talk to them with the harshest tones. You do not want to unload on people in authority over you, so you start unloading on those you love. May God help us. Calvary love is a love that causes us to love. The Lord Jesus caused me to love Him! The more I know Him the more I love Him. The more your wife knows of your love and care for her, the more love she will return to you. Calvary love is a causing love.

CALVARY LOVE IS A CONSTRAINING LOVE

In II Corinthians 5:14 Paul said, *"For the love of Christ constraineth us."* What does this mean? The love of the Lord Jesus stopped me in my tracks. I cannot sin against this love. Calvary love is a constraining love.

It would be wonderful if your wife could say, "I never thought I could live in this life and be married to someone who loves me as you love me and cares for me as you care for me, giving me the attention that you give me." A woman who receives this kind of love is going to be constrained by it. She will find it hard to sin against this kind of love.

This same loving principle works everywhere. For example, it works in the church. A man does not become the pastor of a church and say, "All right, you lucky people, you've got me to love. Now start loving on me." It does not work that way. As the pastor loves his people, buries the aged, marries their young, visits the sick, counsels the troubled, and wins the lost to Christ, the people begin to love him because they know he loves them and is giving his life to them.

There are many women and children who are going in the wrong direction who could be brought to where they should be by the constraining love of Calvary as it is shed abroad from the heart of a husband and father. May God help us to see this. Calvary love is a constraining love.

The two greatest things that men can ever do for their children are to pray for them and love their mother. Through prayer, God can bring influences into their lives that you cannot.

CALVARY LOVE IS A CALMING LOVE

The love of the Lord Jesus calms us. We as Christians are calmed, not by the absence of trouble, but by the presence of the Shepherd. The presence of the Shepherd drives our fears away.

We do not live in a trouble-free world. We live in a dangerous, troubled world. Job 14:1 says, *"Man that is born of a woman is of few days, and full of trouble."* Our hearts are calmed knowing that Christ is near. He is nearer than our hands and feet, closer than our very breath.

This same truth works in the home. Calvary love is a calming love in the home. The Bible says in I John 4:7-11,

> *Beloved, let us love one another: for love is of God; and every one that loveth is born of God, and knoweth God. He that loveth not knoweth not God; for God is love. In this was manifested the love of God toward us, because that God sent his only begotten Son into the world, that we might live through him. Herein is love, not that we loved God, but that he loved us, and sent his Son to be the propitiation for our sins. Beloved, if God so loved us, we ought also to love one another.*

The Bible continues in verses twelve through eighteen,

> *No man hath seen God at any time. If we love one another, God dwelleth in us, and his love is perfected in us. Hereby know we that we dwell in him, and he in us, because he hath given us of his Spirit. And we have seen and do testify that the Father sent the Son to be the Saviour of the world. Whosoever shall confess that Jesus is the Son of God, God dwelleth in him, and he in God. And we have known and believed the love that God hath to us. God is love; and he that dwelleth in love dwelleth in God, and God in him. Herein is our love made perfect, that we may have boldness in the day of judgment: because as he is, so are we in this world. There is no fear in love; but perfect love casteth out fear: because fear hath torment. He that feareth is not made perfect in love.*

Our wives are calmed and our homes are calmed by Calvary love. One of my dearest friends in the ministry shared with me a touching story about his marriage that he has allowed me to repeat. He said, "Years ago, my wife was having a nervous breakdown. To make bad matters worse, when we took her to the doctor, the doctor said to my wife, 'You're going to have to be institutionalized. It is the only way we can help you.' We got back in the car and she began to cry. She turned to me and called my name. With a look of horrible fear and loneliness in her eyes she said, 'You won't put me in a place like that, will you?' I said, 'No, darling. Whatever time it takes, however long it takes, I will stay at home with you until we get you through this.'" He said to me, "Clarence, the healing started the moment I said that." Calvary love has a calming effect on people.

There is so much turmoil in Christian homes when there should be so much peace. Why is there no peace? It is not because children are worried about whether or not they are going to have clothes to wear or whether or not they are going to have food to eat. It is because there is a lack of Calvary love on the part of the husband to calm his wife and to calm his family. The Christian husband should say to his wife, "Honey, God is in control. He has given me grace. We will make it through this. We are going to live. We will be all right. We must be strong in the Lord."

> *There are many women who are going in the wrong direction, and many children who are going in the wrong direction who could be brought to where they should be by the constraining love of Calvary as it is shed abroad from the heart of a husband and father.*

When my sons were small boys, I would say to them on occasion, "I'd like to do something great for God." That was so foolish. Then finally God convicted me, "You are telling those boys the wrong thing." Then I said to my two sons, "I've made a mistake by saying I want to do something great for God. I simply want to be a strong Christian." When I said I wanted to be a strong Christian, immediately God started dealing with me and pointing out to me my weaknesses because His *"strength is made perfect in weakness"* (II Corinthians 12:9).

After these many years of marriage, if my wife did not still believe in what I am trying to do and my children did not believe in the integrity of their dad, I could not even attempt to do what I am doing. I could preach to three or four thousand people in a meeting and have people line up for long periods of time to speak with me, but nothing encourages me as much as my wife turning to me during the drive home and saying, "That was a real blessing to me, honey." If it means that much to me, then I must work at keeping my home a haven, a refuge, and a calm place. Calvary love is a calming love.

CALVARY LOVE IS A CONTINUING LOVE

The strongest thing that could ever be said about marriage was spoken by Jesus Christ. He said in Ephesians 5:25, *"Husbands, love your wives, even as Christ also loved the church, and gave himself for it."* We cannot love our wives to the same degree that the Lord Jesus loves us. It is impossible. But we can love them in the same way.

Here is the way. The Lord Jesus said in Hebrews 13:5, *"I will never leave thee, nor forsake thee."* This is Calvary love, a continuing love. The Lord Jesus did not just go to the cross. He said, "I'm going to bleed and die, be buried, and rise from the dead. This is not all of it. This will get you salvation, but I want you to know I am going to come and dwell in your life forever and take you to heaven when you die. I will never leave you or forsake you." There should be a generation of Christian men who look at their wives and from their hearts, before God, say, "I will never leave thee nor forsake thee. Never!"

Remember the day you stood and someone said to you, "Will you take this woman to be your wedded wife to have and to hold from this day forward, for better, for worse, for richer, for poorer, in sickness and in health, to love and to cherish until death do you part?" Perhaps he asked you to repeat this vow, "I take thee to be my wedded wife, to have and to hold from this day forward, for better, for worse, for richer, for poorer, in sickness and in health, to love and to cherish until death do us part." In the presence of God and the wedding company, you joined your hands together and pledged your lives to God and each other.

Little did we think that day that God would hold us to every part of that vow in our marriages. Two become one and stay together. We are to be as the Lord Jesus is to His church. His arms are always open. He is always ready to receive us, to have us and to hold us.

For better, for worse? We hope for the better, but sometimes there comes the worse. Rich or poor? Sickness or health? Perhaps we never think about being sick. For two years, I could not sleep because of terrible, excruciating nerve pain in my legs. I was developing severe spinal stenosis. The bone on the inside of my spine was pressing against my spinal cord, paralyzing my legs. By degrees, I was losing the use of my legs. When I went to the doctor, he said that something had to be done, but it would take serious surgery.

> *There should be a generation of Christian men who look at their wives and from their hearts, before God, say, "I will never leave thee nor forsake thee. Never!"*

The intensity of the pain increased so rapidly. I went to a neurosurgeon and he said, "If I got your x-rays in an emergency room, I would tell the nurses, 'This man is paralyzed. He cannot walk.' You must have surgery."

I said, "Doctor, my mother is dying and I have to be with my mother. She kept four children together without a husband. Shortly after she and my father were divorced, he died. I am the oldest of those four children. She wants me with her when she dies. I have to be with her. I'll just have to postpone the surgery because I have to be with my mother." I was with my darling mother when she took her last breath. How God strengthened my faith as she looked in the faces of her family and into the face of the Lord Jesus and smiled and went to heaven!

I finally went into a spine institute, and a wonderful Christian surgeon operated on my back. After the surgery, I could not dress myself. I could not bathe myself. I could not care for myself. For a time, I could not do anything. My wife stayed by my side. She had to wash my body. She washed my hair. While I was recovering, I would say several times during the day, "I'm sorry you have to do this. I'm sorry you have to help me." She said, "Darling, I love you, and I love doing this for you. I am happy to do this for you because I love you."

Normally when we talk about intimacy, we talk about the type of intimacy that we all think of immediately. But she and I developed another level of intimacy from the care she gave me, touching me, loving me. We made a promise to God when we were both just kids and were married. We promised, "I will never leave thee or forsake thee. I will love thee in sickness and in health." I never dreamed I would be like a little baby having to be cared for. I thank God she was there to love and minister to me.

We are to be as the Lord Jesus is to His church. His arms are always open. He is always ready to receive us, to have us and to hold us.

One of these days, you will be bent low and if you have not loved and you have not been loved, you are going to be the loneliest man in the world.

It is Calvary love that we must have in the Christian home. Calvary love is a covenant love, a causing love, a calming love, a constraining love, and a continuing love.

Home Work

♦ Keep the covenant you have made with God to be the husband God desires for you to be.

♦ Look after your wife better than she can look after herself.

♦ Speak to your wife gently, not in harsh tones.

♦ Cause your wife to love you more because of your love and care for her.

♦ Love your wife and give her such attention that she feels she cannot sin against your love.

♦ Calm your wife's fears and anxieties by assuring her that God is in control.

♦ Make this commitment to your wife, "I will never leave thee nor forsake thee. Never!"

"Likewise, ye husbands, dwell with them according to knowledge, giving honour unto the wife, as unto the weaker vessel, and as being heirs together of the grace of life; that your prayers be not hindered."

I Peter 3:7

Chapter Five

The Connection Between Home and Heaven

M ost of us have the idea that what we do in our homes has nothing to do with what is taking place in heaven, but this is not so. The Bible says there is a vital connection–a prayer line–between our homes and heaven.

The Bible says in I Peter 3:7, *"Likewise, ye husbands, dwell with them according to knowledge, giving honour unto the wife, as unto the weaker vessel, and as being heirs together of the grace of life; that your prayers be not hindered."* Nothing in the world is any more important than what takes place in the home. There is no place where influence must count for God any more than in the home. There is no place where we are able to exercise as much influence over others for eternity as we are able to do in the home. In this great

verse of Scripture, God deals with the connection between home and heaven.

When Peter wrote this epistle of I Peter under the inspiration of the Spirit of God, he was dealing with an audience that had an entirely different view of marriage than we have today. For instance, during the rule of the Romans, when a wife was caught in adultery, her husband could kill her immediately and no one would say anything about it. If the husband was caught in adultery, his wife could not say a word in opposition to his behavior. For responsibility to be borne by the husband and the wife was something new for them.

THE RESPONSIBILITY OF THE HUSBAND

Both the husband and the wife are to share the privileges of marriage, but both are also to share in the responsibilities of marriage. The Bible says in I Peter 3:1, *"Likewise, ye wives."* Then in verse seven, the Word of God says, *"Likewise, ye husbands."* In this verse of Scripture, we see the responsibility God gives to the husband. The word *"likewise"* makes reference to the Lord Jesus Christ. The husband is to follow the steps of Christ.

God says in I Peter 2:21, *"For even hereunto were ye called: because Christ also suffered for us, leaving us an example, that ye should follow his steps."* Christ has left us an example of behavior. We should follow in His steps. We know that He came to be more than just an example. He came to bleed and die on the cross of Calvary to pay our sin debt. He died, was buried in a borrowed tomb, and rose from the grave, alive forevermore. The Lord Jesus lives forever. By His life, He gave us an example of submission. In I Peter 2:22-25 God's Word says,

> *Who did no sin, neither was guile found in his*
> *mouth: who, when he was reviled, reviled not*

again; when he suffered, he threatened not; but committed himself to him that judgeth righteously: who his own self bare our sins in his own body on the tree, that we, being dead to sins, should live unto righteousness: by whose stripes ye were healed. For ye were as sheep going astray; but are now returned unto the Shepherd and Bishop of your souls.

When we come to the first verse of chapter three, the Bible says, *"Likewise, ye wives."* Peter is making reference to the example of the Lord Jesus. Jesus Christ submitted Himself to the will of the Father. In verse seven of chapter three, when God says, *"Likewise, ye husbands,"* He is making reference to the example of Christ. Every man is to see that Jesus Christ has given us an example.

> *There is no place where we are able to exercise as much influence over others for eternity as we are able to do in the home.*

God's Word commands in Ephesians 5:25, *"Husbands, love your wives, even as Christ also loved the church, and gave himself for it."* The secret to a happy marriage is very simple. The secret is to live a self-giving, self-sacrificing life, not a self-serving life. The Lord Jesus lived a sacrificial life. He was self-giving, not self-serving. We all know people who live for what they can get out of life. They have the idea that everyone has been placed on this earth to do something for them.

The Lord Jesus Christ is an example for both the husband and the wife. In submission to the Father's will, He is an example. He is no less God than God the Father and God the Holy Spirit. Women are no less valuable than men. Christ willingly put

Himself in submission and subjection to God the Father. Wives are to see and follow His example.

The Lord Jesus loved the church and gave Himself for it. We are a part of the church, and we should have no problem yielding to a Savior who loved us enough to give Himself for us.

> *The secret is to live a self-giving, self-sacrificing life, not a self-serving life. The Lord Jesus lived a sacrificial life. He was self-giving, not self-serving.*

A wife would have no problem yielding to a man who loves her enough to give himself for her and to her. Every woman should be submissive to her husband; but she should have the privilege of being submissive to a husband who cares more about her needs than she cares about her own needs. This is the clear teaching of the Word of God. The responsibility of the husband is to care for his wife as Christ cares for the church.

Too many men want to give all the spiritual responsibility in the home to the wife. It is the man's responsibility to be a spiritual leader in the home. The first person out of bed, getting ready to go to God's house, should be the husband, not the wife. The husband should lead in this area.

The Bible says in verse seven, *"Likewise, ye husbands, dwell with them according to knowledge."* Husbands are to make a decision to live with their wives in peace. In Ecclesiastes 9:9 Solomon said, *"Live joyfully with the wife whom thou lovest all the days of the life of thy vanity, which he hath given thee under the sun."*

I thank God for my wife. She has devoted her life to following Christ and making me a happy man. If I cannot be happy at home, I cannot be happy. There is a vital connection between my happiness at home and my heavenly home. We learn from the Word of God that getting along with our wives has everything to do with getting through to God. If we have trouble at home, we cannot get through to God in our prayer lives.

Husbands bear a grave responsibility to dwell with their wives *"according to knowledge."* This means we should study our wives. We should learn what they need, what they love, and what their likes and dislikes are. No two women are exactly alike. Become a student of the wife God has given you. Know what her favorite color is. Know what she likes to wear. We are commanded to dwell with our wives according to knowledge. Some men say, "I'm too busy for that. I have a job to take care of." You had better take care of your home. This is where it all starts. There are many unhappy people who have great careers, but poor unhappy families. God does not intend for it to be this way.

> *Too many men want to give all the spiritual responsibility in the home to the wife. It is the man's responsibility to be a spiritual leader in the home.*

The Word of God says, *"Likewise, ye husbands, dwell with them according to knowledge, giving honour unto the wife."* What does it mean to give honor? It means we are to treat our wives as special treasures from God. Among all the things that I call my own, I am to consider nothing on earth more precious than the treasure of my wife. My wife is my greatest earthly treasure.

I want to be a happy man. Happiness is a heart matter and begins with my relationship to God. My happiness must be demonstrated in my home. If this is to be true, I must bear the responsibility of being a husband. That responsibility begins by taking care of the wife God has given me.

You may say, "I'm married to a woman who likes to look after herself and she doesn't need me." No, you just think she likes to look after herself. God created women with a need to have someone love them, care for them, and treat them with gentleness and love. God created women with a need to be respected, to be considered a precious treasure.

> *Happiness is a heart matter and begins with my relationship to God. My happiness must be demonstrated in my home.*

The Word of God says, *"Likewise, ye husbands, dwell with them according to knowledge, giving honour unto the wife, as unto the weaker vessel."* This *"weaker vessel"* does not have to do with intellect or value, but with the physical being. Sickness can overcome a man, and there are some cases where a woman may be physically stronger than her husband. But, when God deals with the female being, He refers to her as the weaker of the sexes.

I like knowing that my wife needs me to take care of her. Sometimes she brings a jar to me and says, "I can't open the lid." She lets me know that I am needed. It is our responsibility to look after our wives. May God help us to see that the Lord put this in His Word for a purpose.

I am thankful that my wife can drive herself to the store. She can do things on her own, but I still believe she needs me. As the church needs Christ, she needs me. As Christ cares for the church, I am to care for her. We men need to dedicate ourselves to caring for our wives, the precious treasures God has given us.

In the book of Proverbs, we find a powerful verse about words. God follows that verse with a verse about the wife. It is no coincidence that these two verses are together. Many times, we say the harshest things to those we claim to love the most. No one should be taken for granted, much less a wife. The Bible says in Proverbs 18:21, *"Death and life are in the power of the tongue: and they that love it shall eat the fruit thereof."* If we are not careful, we fall into the trap of killing our wives with our tongues. God says this is something we are to avoid. The Bible says in verse twenty-two, *"Whoso findeth a wife findeth a good thing, and obtaineth favour of the LORD."* A wife is a good thing, a precious treasure.

The husband is responsible to *"dwell with them according to knowledge, giving honour unto the wife, as unto the weaker vessel."* This is our God-given assignment. We are to report for duty, accept the assignment, and do our best at it until the Lord Jesus comes.

THE RICHES OF THE CHRISTIAN LIFE

The Bible says in I Peter 3:7, *"Likewise, ye husbands, dwell with them according to knowledge, giving honour unto the wife, as unto the weaker vessel, and as being heirs together of the grace of life."* The Bible says that we are heirs together. Some of us live in spiritual poverty, when God wants us to live with spiritual riches. As husbands and wives, we should do spiritual things together.

God says that we are to marry believers. Saved people should not marry unsaved people. The best way to avoid marrying an unsaved person is not to date an unsaved person. It is scripturally wrong and it is against God to become involved with an unsaved person if you are a Christian. We are not to be unequally yoked together. Christians should date and marry Christians. By following the Word of God, we can avoid a great deal of heartache.

Recently, a man told me that his wife received an inheritance from a relative. With her inheritance, they are going on a cruise together. She is willing to share it with him. They are enjoying their inheritance.

Christians are heirs together of the grace life. If both mates are children of God, they share in the inheritance the Lord gives His children. So many times, we share everything but our spiritual inheritance. When we are saved, we are both children of the same heavenly Father, and we have a spiritual inheritance to share. My wife and I can share things from the Word of God. We can pray together, worship God together, believe the Lord's promises together, sing the songs of the Lord together, and talk about the Lord Jesus together. We should strive to be in harmony spiritually. We have an inheritance to share.

> *There is an intimacy God gives to marriage when we share spiritual things. There are many people whose hearts are yearning to share the Christian life with their spouses.*

There are Christian people who share everything except the things of God. But there is an intimacy God gives to marriage when we share spiritual things. There are many people whose hearts are yearning to share the Christian life with their spouses. The riches of the Christian life can be shared. In your marriage, are you enjoying your salvation?

Years ago, I met a man who was a deacon in a Baptist church. He lived in one end of his house and his wife lived in the other end of the house. Their poor children were caught in the crossfire. No matter what titles that man had in the church, he did not have what God wanted him to have in his life. He did not have peace in his heart or happiness in his home because God does not intend for Christians to live and behave like that.

Both husband and wife should follow the Lord Jesus and love Christ. God says to the husband and wife, "Jesus is your Savior. You have the most precious thing in the world to share together." Determine to be in the house of God with your wife. Determine that you will faithfully attend church with your family. Decide that you are going to share the things of God together. Share all the riches of the Lord Jesus Christ.

THE RESULTS THAT ARE CERTAIN TO FOLLOW

The Bible says, *"Likewise, ye husbands, dwell with them according to knowledge, giving honour unto the wife, as unto the weaker vessel, and as being heirs together of the grace of life; that your prayers be not hindered."* The result of following God's way is that we get our prayers answered.

> *It is a blessed thing to be able to get together as a family and pray and know in your hearts that your prayers are not hindered.*

When was the last time you and your family got together and prayed for the same thing? Do you know why people cannot do that? Many times it is because they are not getting along. It is a blessed thing to be able to get together as a family and pray and know in your hearts that your prayers are not hindered. We will never truly know the hearts of those we love until we hear them speak to God.

It is amazing how God takes one verse and connects all that happens in the home with what takes place in heaven. When we get our homes right, we can get our prayers answered. We can be at peace in the home. There is definitely a connection between the home and heaven.

Home Work

♦ Live a self-sacrificing life, not a self-serving life.

♦ Be the spiritual leader in the home.

♦ Study your wife and learn what she needs, what she loves, and what she likes and dislikes.

♦ Honor your wife and treat her as your most precious earthly treasure.

♦ Share spiritual things with your wife.

♦ Enjoy your salvation together with your wife.

♦ Pray together with your family every day and listen to one another talk to God.

"And I find more bitter than death the woman, whose heart is snares and nets, and her hands as bands: whoso pleaseth God shall escape from her; but the sinner shall be taken by her. Behold, this have I found, saith the preacher, counting one by one, to find out the account: which yet my soul seeketh, but I find not: one man among a thousand have I found; but a woman among all those have I not found. Lo, this only have I found, that God hath made man upright; but they have sought out many inventions."

Ecclesiastes 7:26-29

Chapter Six

Adultery, More Bitter Than Death

 hen I was eighteen years old, the Lord gave me a desire to preach His Word. When I surrendered to His call on my life, I called my pastor and told him that I believed God wanted me to be a preacher. He began immediately giving me counsel about the ministry. One thing I remember him saying was that, when you preach about sin and deal with it openly, you may not see the kind of response you would like to see at the conclusion of the message. He said, "If you follow the Lord, and you preach the truth in the power of the Holy Spirit, God will do His work in the hearts of people in His time."

The Bible says in Ecclesiastes 7:20-29,

> *For there is not a just man upon earth, that doeth good, and sinneth not. Also take no heed*

unto all words that are spoken; lest thou hear thy servant curse thee: for oftentimes also thine own heart knoweth that thou thyself likewise hast cursed others. All this have I proved by wisdom: I said, I will be wise; but it was far from me. That which is far off, and exceeding deep, who can find it out? I applied mine heart to know, and to search, and to seek out wisdom, and the reason of things, and to know the wickedness of folly, even of foolishness and madness: and I find more bitter than death the woman, whose heart is snares and nets, and her hands as bands: whoso pleaseth God shall escape from her; but the sinner shall be taken by her. Behold, this have I found, saith the preacher, counting one by one, to find out the account: which yet my soul seeketh, but I find not: one man among a thousand have I found; but a woman among all those have I not found. Lo, this only have I found, that God hath made man upright; but they have sought out many inventions.

The Word of God says in verse twenty-six, *"More bitter than death."* There is something in life more bitter than death!

This passage deals with the sin of adultery, the sin of getting involved with a strange woman. The Bible word *strange* means "that which does not belong to you." The Word of God says that there is an experience that men have with strange women, women who are not theirs for the taking. This experience is more bitter than death. We need to take this to heart.

Immorality has become epidemic. The guard against it seems to be gone. This experience is more bitter than death.

I must say something about death, because for the Christian, death is not bitter. If you are a Christian dealing with the subject of death, you can find encouragement from God's Word. The Bible says in Revelation 14:13, *"And I heard a voice from heaven saying unto me, Write, Blessed are the dead which die in the Lord from henceforth: yea, saith the Spirit, that they may rest from their labours; and their works do follow them."*

This is a beautiful expression, *"Blessed are the dead which die in the Lord."* Jesus Christ has taken away the sting of death. He suffered our death and hell for us. He was separated from God for us, crying out, *"My God, my God, why hast thou forsaken me?"* He died and was buried and rose from the dead. He said in Revelation 1:18, *"I am he that liveth, and was dead; and, behold, I am alive forevermore."*

> *There is something in life more bitter than death!*

In John 11:25 the Lord Jesus said to the sister of Lazarus, *"I am the resurrection, and the life: he that believeth in me, though he were dead, yet shall he live: and whosoever liveth and believeth in me shall never die."* He then said, *"Believest thou this?"* I want to answer with her, "Yes, Lord, I believe."

If you are a Christian, then death is no more than closing your eyes to time and opening them to eternity. Passing through the door of death into the presence of Jesus Christ will be a greater joy than we can ever imagine on this earth. We will see the face of the Lord Jesus and be with Him forever, where there is no more dying, no more sorrow, and no more death. We can take comfort in the words of Scripture, *"Blessed are the dead which die in the Lord."*

For the man without God, death is bitter. Just as the Bible gives us this expression, it also tells us that there is something that is more bitter than death. Verses twenty and twenty-nine of Ecclesiastes chapter seven serve as bookends for this thought.

The Bible says in verse twenty of Ecclesiastes chapter seven, *"For there is not a just man upon earth, that doeth good, and sinneth not."* The twenty-ninth verse says, *"Lo, this only have I found, that God hath made man upright; but they have sought out many inventions."*

The twentieth verse says that there is not a just man upon the earth. The twenty-ninth verse says that God made man upright in the beginning. If we are going to understand this passage, we need to understand that man is a fallen creature. God made man perfect, but he is a fallen creature and he has a fallen nature. The old nature, left to itself, seeks that which destroys. We need a new nature, because the natural man does not want what is right.

> *If you are a Christian, then death is no more than closing your eyes to time and opening them to eternity.*

When we ask God to forgive our sin and by faith receive the Lord Jesus Christ as Savior, we receive a new nature. We still have the old nature; but once we are saved, we have a new nature. That is why so many Christians live like people who are not Christians; they allow the old nature to rule in their lives. We must learn to get the victory, dying to self and trusting the Lord for spiritual power.

No one is perfect. No one will be perfect until he sees the Lord Jesus. We need the new nature in order to desire right things. The world says, "Live and let live. Let yourself go. Seek pleasure. Feel good. Do it your way." We must remember, as fallen creatures, that our way brings destruction and death.

THE SEARCH

The Bible says in Ecclesiastes 7:20, *"For there is not a just man upon earth, that doeth good and sinneth not."* Then some comments are made about the fact that no one is perfect. Verses twenty-one and twenty-two say, *"Also take no heed unto all words that are spoken; lest thou hear thy servant curse thee: for oftentimes also thine own heart knoweth that thou thyself likewise hast cursed others."* We are quick to condemn other people. We need to look in the mirror and see that we are guilty of the same things.

The Bible says in verse twenty-three, *"All this have I proved by wisdom: I said, I will be wise; but it was far from me."* Solomon said, "I want to know everything. I want all the answers. I want to search out every matter." But he could not have perfect knowledge. The Bible says in verses twenty-four and twenty-five, *"That which is far off, and exceeding deep, who can find it out? I applied my heart to know, and to search, and to seek out wisdom, and the reason of things, and to know the wickedness of folly, even of foolishness and madness."* The man said, "I'm on a search." We are all on a search. Sometimes I hear people say, "I don't care what I do. I don't care what I become." This is not true. We are all searching. Someone has said that all mankind is searching for significance. We want to make our place. We desire fame and recognition.

All mankind is searching for security. Some people have the idea that if they make enough money and put enough money somewhere, that they can be secure; or if they can surround themselves with the right kind of people or get the right kind of employment, they can be secure.

We are also searching for satisfaction. When we take significance, security, and satisfaction, and apply the search for these to the old nature, we see how wild people can become in their searching and how far off course they can go trying to find these things.

If a man who had all the money in the world walked into a doctor's office and was told that he had only days to live, his money would not help him. The only real security and safety is in the Lord Jesus Christ. Our satisfaction is in the Lord Jesus Christ. This is what we are dealing with, in large part, in the book of Ecclesiastes.

> *The only real security and safety is in the Lord Jesus Christ.*

Remember that we are fallen people. If we throw the reins of our lives to the wind and say, "I'll do whatever I feel like doing," we are headed on a course of self-destruction that will bring hurt, ruin, and harm to us and many others.

Solomon was searching. The search is on in every one of our lives. I hope and pray that you have come to the place where you have realized that the search should end at the feet of the Lord Jesus Christ. You will find in Him all that you ever need.

THE SNARE

As we read on in chapter seven, verse twenty-six, the Bible says, *"And I find more bitter than death the woman, whose heart is snares."* Solomon said, "I haven't found out everything, but I have found out one thing, I have found out that there is an evil relationship that you can get involved in that is more bitter than death."

The Bible says, *"I find more bitter than death the woman, whose heart is snares and nets, and her hands as bands."* He had in mind the visual image of an animal being caught. He is speaking of a snare set for a helpless bird. He said, "Her heart is like a snare." A man may think, "I'm masculine, I'm strong, I'm making the decisions, I'm doing what I want to do, I'm doing as I please and I'm getting involved where I want to get involved." God says, "No, you are like a little bird walking into a snare."

The Bible says, *"...and her hands as bands."* God says her hands are like chains. Those dainty little hands soon become chains of iron to hold onto you. Solomon said that he had learned this.

He went on to say that in a thousand women, he could not find one that satisfied. Here is a man who could have anything and everything. The Bible says in I Kings 11:3, *"And he had seven hundred wives, princesses, and three hundred concubines: and his wives turned away his heart."* One thousand women, can you imagine? On second thought, do not try to imagine. You may have a hard enough time trying to keep up with one!

The Bible says in Ecclesiastes 7:27-28, *"Behold, this have I found, saith the preacher, counting one by one, to find out the account: which yet my soul seeketh, but I find not: one man among a thousand have I found; but a woman among all those have I not found."* The primary interpretation of this verse is the fact that as Solomon looked in his own court among his own friends, he said, "I cannot find a good man." There is only One that is perfect. There is only One who ever lived that is all right. That One is the God-Man, the Lord Jesus Christ.

Solomon said here, "When I looked upon a thousand women, I found none." You might think he was being pretty hard on women. The man was saying, "I tried to find what my life needed in women; in a thousand, and I did not find it."

You think you have her, but she has you. You think you have ensnared her, but she has ensnared you. You think she is in your net and you can take her anywhere you wish, but you are in her net and she will lead you around. You love her feminine little hands, but they are soon chains of iron.

What you find in that experience is what you thought was going to be something beyond your fondest dreams, but you found out in the end that it is *"more bitter than death."* The man who runs after a strange woman is going to learn that his experience is more bitter than death.

I have said many times that nothing on earth, outside of Jesus Christ, can make a man rise any higher than a good woman. Nothing can make a man be all he should be like a good woman. It is beautiful. It is wonderful. Many men have risen above where they ever dreamed they would rise because of a good woman. The kind of woman you want to be at home with your children, that you want your children to admire and love, should be the kind of woman you want to come home to every day. Some men practice a double standard that is destructive.

If nothing can make a man rise higher on earth than a good, decent woman, then nothing can bring a man down so low as a woman who is not what God meant for her to be.

The Bible says in the fifth chapter of Proverbs, verses five through nine,

> *Her feet go down to death; her steps take hold*
> *on hell. Lest thou shouldest ponder the path of life,*
> *her ways are moveable, that thou canst not know*
> *them. Hear me now therefore, O ye children, and*
> *depart not from the words of my mouth. Remove*
> *thy way far from her, and come not nigh the door*
> *of her house: lest thou give thine honour unto*
> *others, and thy years unto the cruel.*

Perhaps you are thinking of someone who once was an honorable man but is not now. People once thought highly of him but do not now, because he let a woman bring him down. Everyone who has lived long enough to be an adult has examples racing through his mind of people he knows who fall into this category.

The Bible goes on to say in verses ten through thirteen of Proverbs chapter five,

> *Lest strangers be filled with thy wealth; and thy labours be in the house of a stranger; and thou mourn at the last, when thy flesh and thy body are consumed, and say, How have I hated instruction, and my heart despised reproof; and have not obeyed the voice of my teachers, nor inclined mine ear to them that instructed me!*

Solomon compares this strange woman with the wife one should be faithful to and love. The Bible says in verse fifteen, *"Drink waters out of thine own cistern, and running waters out of thine own well."* Of course, this is a proverb meaning, "Find your pleasure and satisfaction at home, not out somewhere else." Verses sixteen through eighteen say, *"Let thy fountains be dispersed abroad, and rivers of waters in the streets. Let them be only thine own, and not strangers' with thee. Let thy fountain be blessed: and rejoice with the wife of thy youth."*

> *The man who runs after a strange woman is going to learn that his experience is more bitter than death.*

Verses twenty through twenty-two say,

> *And why wilt thou, my son, be ravished with a
> strange woman, and embrace the bosom of a
> stranger? For the ways of man are before the
> eyes of the* LORD, *and he pondereth all his goings.
> His own iniquities shall take the wicked himself,
> and he shall be holden with the cords of his sins.*

You may be saying, "I am in charge." No, before long, sin
becomes the master and you become the slave. I know men of
means, men of wealth, men of power, men of prestige, men of
popularity, who are supporting half a dozen women. They have
found that their fun turned into an experience that is more bitter
than death. Verse twenty-three says, *"He shall die without
instruction; and in the greatness of his folly he shall go astray."*

I once spoke to a man about a well-known businessman he knew.
I said, "Where is he now?" He said, "He is bagging groceries at the
market." I asked what had happened to him and the reply was, "A
woman got him. He lost his business, he lost his home, he lost his
wealth, he lost everything. He took up with a young woman in the
office. It started out as fun, but now everything is gone."

We are living in an immoral society. We are no longer
shocked to hear about preachers or government leaders who live
immoral lives. What about the man who is now bagging bread,
who could have owned a chain of stores? I will tell you what
happened to him. The Bible says in Proverbs 6:26, *"For by
means of a whorish woman a man is brought to a piece of
bread: and the adulteress will hunt for the precious life."*

Am I down on women? No, but I am trying to warn some
men and women. I have been into too many homes trying to put
them back together. If I had only been in one, it would be too
many. The attitude of the day is to do as you please. You will
find that this lifestyle is more bitter than death.

THE SAFETY

We have considered the search, the snare, and now the safety. The Bible says in Ecclesiastes 7:26, *"And I find more bitter than death the woman, whose heart is snares and nets, and her hands as bands: whoso pleaseth God shall escape from her; but the sinner shall be taken by her."*

Notice that word, *"escape."* Remember the snare of an adulterous relationship. If you are married and sexually involved with another person, you are an adulterer or an adulteress. If you are unmarried, you are a whoremonger. This is a strong word. Perhaps if we used stronger language, we would have less activity like this. You may say, "This is just an affair, a thrill, a casual meeting that turned into more." No, you are a whoremonger or an adulterer.

If you think because you are a Christian and part of a Bible-believing church, you are automatically exempt from this kind of thing, you are wrong. Most of us have friends that we have known and loved for years, even ministers, who are no longer in the ministry because of immorality. This grieves our hearts. It grieves our hearts not only for them, but also for everyone involved. There is so much heartache with which their families must deal.

There is no safety in simply saying, "Well, I am going to resist." This is part of it, but our safety has much more to do with our nearness to God than our distance from the opposite sex.

The Bible says in Ecclesiastes 7:26, *"Whoso pleaseth God shall escape from her."* You may think this means that you will please God if you do not get involved with a strange woman. But it means that, if a man is pleasing God with his life, he will not go out looking for a *"strange woman."* This will not happen if a man is pleasing God with his life.

If you hear of a preacher who falls, he did not fall with the woman first. He fell first in his walk with God. If he had not fallen in his walk with God, he would not have fallen with the woman. If you are a Christian and you get involved in an immoral relationship, the first fall is not that of the immoral relationship. The first fall is the coldness you allowed into your heart by falling from fellowship with God. This is why it troubles me when people begin missing church. I like coming to church to have my heart stirred and to be reminded of right things. When we become casual about the way we attend church, we are setting ourselves up to let things come between us and our Lord and His church. There is safety only in Jesus Christ. May God help us to always feel hurt when we hear about the fallen.

Some may say, "My problem is not another woman or another man." Whatever the problem is, the only way to get the victory, the only way of safety, is in nearness to Jesus Christ.

In Proverbs 16:6 the Bible says, *"By mercy and truth iniquity is purged: and by the fear of the LORD men depart from evil."* Solomon said, "I haven't learned everything, but I have learned from a thousand women that you don't find complete satisfaction in any one of them." God has designed life so that the greatest fulfillment and satisfaction can only be found in the Person of Jesus Christ. Solomon learned that the only place to escape and the only place of safety is in pleasing God. As we please God, we flee from wrong things.

May God protect me. By His grace, I praise Him that He has. I am a human being. I have an old nature. But I want to walk with God. I want to finish the course that He has given me. I want to run the race. I want to look Him in the face some day and say, "Lord, I made a covenant with You about my wife and I have kept it." I want you to pray that I will do that. By His grace, I intend to do that.

Let us pray that in our churches the Lord will raise up strong families who will never taste this experience that is more bitter than death.

Home Work

♦ Stay near to God so you can resist temptations.

♦ Fellowship with the Lord daily and do not let your heart become cold towards Him.

♦ Be faithful to attend church to keep your heart stirred to live right.

♦ Realize that our greatest fulfillment and satisfaction can only be found in the Person of Jesus Christ.

♦ Keep the covenant you have made with God and be faithful to your spouse.

*"Children's children are the crown of old men;
and the glory of children are their fathers."*

Proverbs 17:6

Chapter Seven

Fathers, the Glory of Children

As we read the Bible, we discover that the Lord places a tremendous emphasis on the home. The word *mother* is found in the Bible 363 times, but we find the word *father* mentioned more than 1,300 times. God has a message for fathers.

The Bible says in Proverbs 17:6, *"Children's children are the crown of old men; and the glory of children are their fathers."*

What a wonderful expression, *"children's children."* They are the *"crown of old men."* Take special note of the expression, *"the glory of children."* The Word of God says, *"The glory of children are their fathers."*

We are living in a world where millions of children have no glory. For the most part, my father considered his profession to be gambling. He certainly did not do all the things he should have done as a father. However, he tried to teach me noteworthy things about life.

Often my father would say to me, "When you shake hands, shake hands firmly. When you speak to people, look them in the eye." He said to me again and again, "When a lady walks into the room, stand to greet her. When you are greeting someone older than you, stand up to show respect and greet him." He said, "Your word is your bond. If you say you are going to do something, do it. If you give a man your word, keep it."

> *We are living in a world where millions of children have no glory.*

My father taught me to answer, "Yes, sir" and "No, sir;" "Yes, ma'am" and "No, ma'am." The rule around our house was, "Do not talk back to your mother." These are good things, but the best things concern our relationship and fellowship with the Lord Jesus Christ.

General Douglas MacArthur said, "When I am gone, I do not want to be remembered as a great general. I want to be remembered as a Christian father who read the Bible and prayed with his children." What a hero!

FATHERS SHOULD BE CHRISTIANS

In order for children to glory in their fathers, their fathers must be Christians. Every child should know that his daddy has trusted the Lord Jesus Christ as his Savior. Christ died for our sin and rose from the dead. To be a Christian, we must confess to God that we are sinners and trust in the finished work of Christ for salvation.

Our children should know we are Christians; not because we go to church, carry a Bible, or say we are saved; but because of the way we behave in our homes. They should know we are saved by the way we respond to problems, by the way we treat their mothers, and by the change Jesus Christ has made in our lives.

FATHERS SHOULD HAVE BIBLE-BASED CONVICTIONS

Fathers must have convictions. Children should know where Dad stands on the issues of life. Be courageous enough to stand your ground; let your children know you are a man of integrity by the way you live. Dad, speak freely and often of your convictions. Be courageous.

FATHERS SHOULD LIVE CLEAN LIVES

If you have habits you do not want your children to have, ask God

General Douglas MacArthur said, "When I am gone, I do not want to be remembered as a great general. I want to be remembered as a Christian father who read the Bible and prayed with his children." What a hero!

to give you the victory over them. If you have reading material in your home you would not want your children to read, get it out of your home. Children should never find that Daddy is doing anything that makes them ashamed to say, "That's my dad." If your children see you watching something on television involving profanity or nudity, something happens to their glory. Remember, *"The glory of children are their fathers."*

In the book of I Samuel, we find the story of a priest named Eli. He had two sons, Hophni and Phinehas. They were to be the spiritual leaders of Israel, but they were not. The Israelites went to battle against the Philistines, and in that battle over thirty thousand Israelites lost their lives including Eli's sons.

> *Our children should know we are Christians; not because we go to church, or carry a Bible, or say we are saved; but because of the way we behave in our homes.*

The Philistines took the ark of the covenant, which represented the presence of the Lord. Word reached Eli that not only had the ark been taken, but thirty thousand people were dead, including his sons. When the old man heard the news, he fell backward, broke his neck, and died. As Phinehas' wife gave birth to a child, she gave this child a meaningful name. The Bible says in I Samuel 4:21-22, *"And she named the child Ichabod, saying, The glory is departed from Israel: because the ark of God was taken, and because of her father in law and her husband. And she said, The glory is departed from Israel: for the ark of God is taken."* Note the expression, *"The glory is departed."* She named the child Ichabod, indicating, *"The glory is departed."*

Where does a nation find her glory? She finds it in her people. Where do her people find their glory? The Bible says that children find their glory in their fathers. Where do fathers find their glory? They must find their glory in God.

When fathers do not glory in God, the children find no glory in their fathers. As a result, the nation finds no glory in her children. We are a nation with fewer and fewer people finding glory in God, and we can find no glory in our children. The Bible says that the glory of children is their fathers. If you are a father, your heart should be stirred. You should say, "God helping me, I am going to be all I should be and can be for the Lord and for the good of my children."

The Bible says in Proverbs 17:6, *"Children's children are the crown of old men."* I love my grandchildren. I thank God for them. Of course, they are special. While I am rejoicing, looking down at the children, the children are looking up at me. Every child needs to glory in his father. This tremendous responsibility is given to the father.

> *When fathers do not glory in God, the children find no glory in their fathers. As a result, the nation finds no glory in her children.*

CHILDREN GLORY IN THE LEADERSHIP OF THEIR FATHERS

God has called the father to be the leader of the home. When you hold a little boy in your arms, that child is destined for leadership. God has designed the family so that the father is to lead. Mother should be the greatest encouragement for Father to lead. In some circumstances, a mother must lead. This could be because of the absence of the father, or the neglect or sin of the father; but God has designed the father to lead.

At the end of the book of Joshua, we find Joshua at 110 years of age standing on the threshold of eternity. He is looking back across his life. He was born in Egypt of the tribe of Ephraim.

He was stirred about what God had done in his life. The Bible says in Joshua 24:15,

> *And if it seem evil unto you to serve the LORD, choose you this day whom ye will serve; whether the gods which your fathers served that were on the other side of the flood, or the gods of the Amorites, in whose land ye dwell: but as for me and my house, we will serve the LORD.*

Notice, it was not Joshua's wife who jumped up in front of the crowd and said, "I want to tell you boys something!" Watching some women, you would think it might happen that way. I am not against women. I am simply for God's way of leadership in the home.

Something is terribly wrong with a nation whose women do so much leading. To see manhood disappearing is evidence of spiritual illness. Men do not need to look like women. Men should look like men, distinctively different from women. They do not need to be bejeweled and decorated as women are decorated.

> *To see manhood disappearing is evidence of spiritual illness.*

Joshua, a real man, stood up and said, "I am speaking for my house." He took the leadership. Children should be able to glory in the leadership of their fathers. They should be able to say, "Daddy is leading. We know where he stands, we know what he believes, and we know what he teaches. He is the leader." Children should have the leadership of their fathers in which to glory. Joshua said, *"As for me and my house, we will serve the LORD."*

We all sin and come short of the glory of God. We all have feet of clay. We should not pretend to be perfect, but it is the

man's responsibility to lead. The more closely we follow Jesus
Christ, the better leaders we will become.

In Ephesians chapter five, the Lord Jesus Christ gave these
words to the apostle Paul to pen about the church and the home.
The Bible says in Ephesians 5:21-23,

> *Submitting yourselves one to another in the
> fear of God. Wives, submit yourselves unto your
> own husbands, as unto the Lord. For the husband
> is the head of the wife, even as Christ is the head
> of the church: and he is the saviour of the body.*

The Bible says that the husband is the head of the wife, just
as Christ is the head of the church. He is to be the leader.
Because my parents divorced when I was a child, I was reared
by my mother, a strong woman. My mother had to be strong. I
believe she learned how to be strong in the furnace of conflict,
in a life of difficulty. But remember, it is the responsibility of
Dad to lead his family.

CHILDREN GLORY IN THE LOVE OF THEIR FATHERS

God's Word says we are to love one another. Men are to love
their wives and love the Lord.

If you want to know whether or not a man should be tender
and compassionate, look at Christ. We are to be like Him, and
He is tender and compassionate. Children need to see this love
in the lives of their fathers. Love is firm. Love is committed.
Love is tenacious. Love takes hold and holds on. Fathers need
to say, "I am not going to lose my children. I am not going to
lose my wife. I am not going to lose my family. I am going to
hang on and do what is necessary." Love is tough.

Love is also very tender. Most men need to work on being more expressive and tender. Perhaps we have gone so overboard with the idea of toughness in men that we have become like machines with no heart. Jesus Christ wept. He touched. He held children in His arms. He was approachable. No one ever doubted that He loved. Children should be able to glory in the love of their fathers.

We especially need to be able to lead our children to Jesus Christ. We should set a goal early in our children's lives that we want to see them come to know Christ as their Savior. This goal should be expressed foremost by praying for their salvation.

Some parents do a better job taking care of and training their pets than they do their children. They say to their dog, "Roll over," and he rolls over. They say to their dog, "Sit up," and he sits up. They say to their dog, "Stick out your paw and shake hands," and he sticks out his paw and shakes hands, but they cannot get their children to obey much of anything. When the dog is better behaved than the children, something is wrong.

We all have a rebellious nature, and children are naturally going to rebel against authority. How deep the pain and the hurt is when the rebellion comes, and the father must face God with the fact that he has not loved and cared for his children as he could have. Children should glory in the leadership and love of their fathers. Fathers, lead your children to Christ and into a life of obedience to the Lord.

CHILDREN GLORY IN THE LOYALTY OF THEIR FATHERS

Fathers should be loyal to Christ. If children believe that their fathers love Jesus Christ first and foremost, they can glory in this. Can your children say, "My daddy is a spiritual man. My daddy is going to do right because he loves the Lord, and he has promised God that he is going to do right"? Give your children the opportunity to glory in your loyalty to Christ.

There will be times in life when as fathers we will have opportunity to prove our integrity, our decency, our honesty, and our loyalty to Christ. There will come crises in life when God gives us opportunities, in the eyes of our children, to prove what Christ means to us. If we cut corners, our hearts will be broken later.

I will never forget an old story of a preacher whose children brought home a dog. The rightful owner of the dog heard that the animal had strayed into the preacher's yard. They called to see if he indeed had their dog. Over the phone they identified their dog as having a few white hairs in his tail. The preacher said, "This dog looks just like yours, but it is not your dog." Then the preacher, along with his sons, pulled the white hairs out of the dog's tail that would have identified

> *We should set a goal early in our children's lives that we want to see them come to know Christ as their Savior. This goal should be expressed foremost by praying for their salvation.*

him to his owner. Later in life, one of those sons said, "I do not serve God because there was a day when my father betrayed his honesty and integrity. He lied about a little lost dog, and I lost confidence in him." Perhaps that was only an excuse; but nevertheless, children should be able to glory in the loyalty that their fathers have to Christ.

Children should also be able to glory in the loyalty that their fathers have to the family. Fathers, we should be loyal to our families, wives, and children. In the world there is much temptation. Someone is always trying to turn our heads. But the Bible says in Proverbs 6:26, *"For by means of a whorish woman a man is brought to a piece of bread."* What may seem to be something innocent when you are discouraged or have had a bad day at home is, in truth, anything but innocent. It will lead you to a place of no return. If you continue in the sin of adultery, you will never again be what you should be.

> *Children should be able to glory in the loyalty of their fathers to Christ, to the family, and to the church.*

A father must say, "By the grace of God, I am going to be loyal to my family." We must stand before the Lord and say, "Lord, I make this covenant. I promise to be a loyal husband and father." We have a world of confused children today, because they do not know who their daddy loves. It certainly does not appear to be their mother. People survive, and somehow they seem to deal with it; but we have sown to the wind, and we are reaping the whirlwind.

Children should be able to glory in the loyalty of their fathers to Christ, to the family, and to the church. You should attend your church faithfully. Your children should know that the whole family will be in church Sunday morning, Sunday evening, and Wednesday evening. However, loyalty is more than attendance; it is an attitude.

When you leave the church services, are you still loyal? Fathers, in your conversations with your family, as you talk about Sunday School teachers, the pastor, workers, and leaders; are your children able to glory in your loyalty to the church? This is very important.

The home is under a terrible attack. The Devil seems to have almost free reign in certain places. Hardly a week goes by that I do not hear about some home being ripped apart, ravaged by sin. What does this do to the children? They lose their glory.

The first revival meeting I ever conducted was in a small country church. Every night in that meeting, a well-dressed lady in her fifties would come. Her husband attended the services with her, but he was not a Christian.

> *Dad, please consider what it could mean to your family if you loved the Lord as you should love Him now, if you served Him as you should serve Him now.*

They had a son who was saved. Every night of the meeting we prayed for the father's salvation. Every time the invitation was given, someone came to the altar and prayed for the father to be saved. It seemed that the burden and goal of the entire church was to see that family together in Christ.

If you had met the wife and mother, you would understand that she was an exemplary Christian, and the son was a fine Christian boy. All that was necessary to make a beautiful Christian home was the salvation of the father. As strange as it may sound, the man even tithed to the church. He supported everything going on, but he did not know the Lord as his Savior.

The revival meeting concluded, and the man did not get saved. Not long after that, the son was involved in a terrible automobile accident and was killed. When I went to the funeral service, I learned that through the accident and death of his son, the father came to Christ. The comment was made, "We will be together in heaven now." I rejoiced, but I also thought, "How good it would have been for them to have been together in Christ on earth as well."

Children will not be young for long. They are grown and gone before we know it. Dad, please consider what it could mean to your family if you loved the Lord as you should love Him now, if you served Him as you should serve Him now. Father, it would be wonderful if your children could glory in your leadership, your love, and your loyalty now. May God in heaven help us to do what is right.

Home Work

♦ Know that you have trusted Christ by faith as your Savior.

♦ Behave like a Christian in your home.

♦ Have Bible-based convictions and speak about them often.

♦ Live such a clean life that your children will never be ashamed of you.

♦ Take the responsibility of being the leader in your home.

♦ Work on expressing your love tenderly to your wife and children.

♦ Pray for the salvation of your children.

♦ Lead your children to Christ and into a life of obedience to Him.

♦ Be loyal to Christ, to your wife, to your children, to your church, and to your pastor.

"Who can find a virtuous woman? for her price is far above rubies."

Proverbs 31:10

Chapter Eight

A Virtuous Woman

 he Bible asks in Proverbs chapter thirty-one and verse ten, *"Who can find a virtuous woman? for her price is far above rubies."* What a question!

We are living in a world that has gone through tremendous changes in recent years. We have witnessed a revolution of moral values. Loosed from our original moorings, we are drifting as a nation.

America is not the nation she was a generation ago. Much of the blame lies in the lack of true manhood. We need faithful men in our churches who will lead their families and stand up for what they believe.

Along with an awful attack upon manhood, an equally fierce attack is being waged upon women and biblical womanhood.

Women are being deceived. They are believing the Devil's lie and trading their honored place of God's design for a place of dishonor in the Devil's plan.

There is nothing quite as precious or treasured on earth, humanly speaking, as a virtuous woman. Christian women should be determined to set a holy example for those who follow after them. Who can find a virtuous woman?

> *Christian women should be determined to set a holy example for those who follow after them. Who can find a virtuous woman?*

Proverbs 31 begins, *"The words of king Lemuel, the prophecy that his mother taught him."* All through the book of Proverbs, we have the idea that a father is teaching his son. When we come to this last chapter of Proverbs, God says these are the words of a mother given to her son, King Lemuel.

We know very little about this king. We know his name; perhaps this is a name used for someone else. Some writers even believe it to be Solomon. I do not have a certain answer to this question, but I do know that King Lemuel is mentioned here and his mother is teaching him.

She declares in verse two, *"What, my son? and what, the son of my womb? and what, the son of my vows?"* She said, "You are not only my son, you are the son of my womb; and not only the son of my womb, but the son of my vows. I've vowed to God, I've made a covenant with God for you! I received you from God." This reminds us of Hannah, the mother of Samuel. She prayed for a son that she would give back to the Lord, and she kept her promise.

If you study Old Testament history, you will discover that the son born to Hannah was the man God used to bring about a mighty revival in Israel. The land was torn apart until the prophet Samuel stepped on the scene and started schools of the prophets. He began teaching people the Word of God and bringing them back to the Lord. If we had more Hannahs, we would have more Samuels. Many men have chased after wild women only to think later that they would not want that kind of woman to be the mother of their children.

King Lemuel's mother began to teach him by saying in verses three through five, *"Give not thy strength unto women, nor thy ways to that which destroyeth kings. It is not for kings, O Lemuel, it is not for kings to drink wine; nor for princes strong drink: lest they drink, and forget the law, and pervert the judgment of any of the afflicted."*

> *There is nothing quite as precious or treasured on earth, humanly speaking, as a virtuous woman.*

She said, "You should not let liquor capture you. Keep it from your lips. Avoid running after women, and stay away from liquor." This sounds like a godly mother, does it not? Then she asked in verse ten, *"Who can find a virtuous woman?"* She goes on to describe a virtuous woman in this beautiful portrait of words.

THE HEART OF THE VIRTUOUS WOMAN

"Who can find a virtuous woman? for her price is far above rubies." Her heart is priced far above rubies. She said, "Son, I want you to be more concerned about what a woman is than what a woman has done or has accomplished. I want you to be more concerned about her character than her accomplishments."

This is a day in which we praise people for what they have accomplished. This godly mother told her son he should look at the heart if he wanted a virtuous woman. Virtue is one of the things we should consider. Thinking on virtue can be life-changing. The Bible says in Philippians 4:8 that it will do us good just to think about virtue. *"Who can find a virtuous woman?"*

The Bible tells us in II Peter 1:4, *"Whereby are given unto us exceeding great and precious promises: that by these ye might be partakers of the divine nature, having escaped the corruption that is in the world through lust."*

If you desire to know what is exactly opposite of a virtuous life, notice the expression, *"Having escaped the corruption that is in the world through lust."*

> *Virtue is not trying to be like someone else, but it is allowing the indwelling Christ to take control and make us like Him from the inside.*

The Bible says in II Peter 1:5, *"And beside this, giving all diligence, add to your faith...."* This passage is speaking to those of us who have already trusted the Lord Jesus Christ as our personal Savior. We do not add faith, we add to our faith!

Faith becomes the foundation. There are graces which we are to add to our faith. There are seven of these graces–virtue, knowledge, temperance, patience, godliness, brotherly kindness, and charity–but the very first thing God says to add is virtue. Virtue is what we are by God's grace by trusting in the indwelling Holy Spirit to produce Christlikeness in us.

Virtue has to do with character–Christian character, godly character, Christlikeness. Out of virtue comes honesty; out of virtue comes truth and purity.

Virtue becomes a garden from which other desirable qualities bloom and grow. The most Christ-like characteristic we find is virtue. It is a heart matter. Virtue is not trying to be like someone else, but it is allowing the indwelling Christ to take control and make us like Him from the inside.

God says men need to find a virtuous woman. She is a woman who has a heart for God, whose heart is changed, who wants to live a holy life from the inside; because it is what God wants for her. *"Who can find a virtuous woman?"*

A virtuous woman is someone who does not argue about what is right. She is someone who loves Christ. As soon as she finds out what Christ wants, she does it. *"Who can find a virtuous woman?"* Many things are said about the appearance of women; but when we talk about the outward appearance, we need to realize that it all starts in the heart.

In I Timothy 2:9 the Bible says, *"In like manner also, that women adorn themselves in modest apparel, with shamefacedness, and sobriety."*

We live in an immodest age. This is a day when the blush is gone, when almost nothing embarrasses people. The sensitivity of womanhood to immodesty has been lost in our country.

Tell me where we can find a virtuous woman dressed in modest apparel. The answer is among God's people. We should not be so affected by the world. The truth is, if there is virtue in the heart of a Christian woman, she will not have a desire to dress immodestly. This might be hard for some people to swallow, but I believe it is the truth. If there is virtue in the heart of a Christian woman, she will want to adorn herself in modest apparel; not to be seen of men or to turn the heads of men, but to honor God.

Titus 2:3-5 states,

> *The aged women, likewise, that they be in behaviour as becometh holiness, not false accusers, not given to much wine, teachers of good things; that they may teach the young women to be sober, to love their husbands, to love their children, to be discreet, chaste, keepers at home, good, obedient to their own husbands, that the word of God be not blasphemed.*

> *We live in an immodest age. This is a day when the blush is gone, when almost nothing embarrasses people. The sensitivity of womanhood to immodesty has been lost in our country.*

Older women have a charge from the Lord to provide the right example for the younger women. Virtue in the heart will produce modesty in appearance. Tell me, what do you want for your daughters? What do you want for your granddaughters? God said the aged women should set the example. If you have clothing that you would consider to be immodest, you should get rid of it.

A person with virtue does not argue about what to wear when it comes to being modest or immodest. It is a heart matter. You may think modesty has nothing to do with appearance, but it has everything to do with it. God looks on the heart, but man looks on the outward appearance. We dress a certain way because we are a certain way in our hearts.

The Bible says in Proverbs 7:8-10,

> *Passing through the street near her corner; and he went the way to her house, in the twilight, in the evening, in the black and dark night: and, behold, there met him a woman with the attire of an harlot, and subtil of heart.*

God says that this woman was dressed in the attire of a harlot. Why would God say she was dressed like a harlot? Her clothing revealed things about her body that should not have been emphasized.

We live in a world where everything from soap to jeans is sold by sex. You want to buy a new car? A girl comes with it. At least, you would think so if you watched the advertisement.

> *The further this world goes to the left, the more extreme our Bible position sounds.*

We are being sold a lie. Why are homes breaking up at a greater rate than ever before? Why are people fouling out of life? Why do people laugh at the biblical position of abstinence before marriage? Because of our disease-ridden population, abstinence is gaining some ground, but God declared it was right to wait until after marriage long before there was a fear of AIDS.

The further this world goes to the left, the more extreme our Bible position sounds. Right is still right; the Bible is still the Bible; virtue is still virtue; modesty is still modesty. *"Who can find a virtuous woman?"*

THE HUSBAND OF A VIRTUOUS WOMAN

"The heart of her husband doth safely trust in her, so that he shall have no need of spoil." Proverbs 31:11

Her husband trusts her. You cannot build a home without trust. If you are married to a woman you cannot trust, you will be miserable. If you are married to a woman who is constantly attempting to turn the heads of men, you will be miserable. If you are married to a woman who is constantly coming on to men, you will be miserable.

Every virtuous wife deserves a God-fearing, God-honoring, Spirit-filled husband; and every Christian man deserves a virtuous wife that he can trust. God's Word says, *"Her husband doth safely trust in her."*

In Proverbs 12:4 the Bible says, *"A virtuous woman is a crown to her husband: but she that maketh ashamed is as rottenness in his bones."*

The Bible says that a virtuous woman is a crown to her husband, but a woman who is not virtuous makes her husband ashamed and is as rottenness in his bones. Wives, if you want to have a happy husband, be what the Bible calls a virtuous woman.

The world has caused us to believe that being virtuous is synonymous with being seedy, ugly, and withdrawn. The world wants to give the idea that the only pretty girls are the ones running around on a beerwagon, hopping from bar to bar with a bottle of booze, half-clad. They do not show you the end of that lifestyle. They do not show you a life wrecked and ruined. They do not show you the destruction of a home. They do not show you a drunken wife coming home. They do not show you the disease, death, and all the heartache that goes along with that lifestyle.

The finished product of the brewer's art is not a bottle of ice-cold beer in a lovely woman's hand. The finished product of a brewer's art is a wrecked and ruined life, a broken home, and cursed children.

We need virtuous mothers who will teach their sons to look for the right thing in the women they are going to marry, and that is a heart of virtue. Men, you have no right to pray for a virtuous wife if you are not willing to be a virtuous husband.

How I thank God for a virtuous wife! I am thankful to come home to her. I can trust her, and I love her! This is the way it should be. She is a crown to my life. If you have a virtuous wife, tell her you love her and that you are thankful for her. Who can find one?

> *The finished product of a brewer's art is a wrecked and ruined life, a broken home, and cursed children.*

Some say, "I've made some mistakes." Others say, "People think I've made mistakes, but someone else has made a mess of my life." Forget it. If you have trusted Christ as your Savior, God has forgotten your sin. If you have asked the Lord to forgive your sin and by faith you have received Christ as your Savior, your sin is gone. Your sin is cast behind the back of the Lord, buried in the depths of the sea, removed as far as the east is from the west.

I pray to God that we will be so filled with the Holy Spirit that, by our appearance, people will know we are Christians. Let me tell you who the most beautiful people in the world are. They are men and women who by spending time with God have the beauty of the Lord. Psalm 90:17 says, *"And let the beauty of the LORD our God be upon us."*

THE HOME OF A VIRTUOUS WOMAN

What about her home? The Bible says in Proverbs 31:12-15,

> *She will do him good and not evil all the days of her life. She seeketh wool, and flax, and worketh willingly with her hands. She is like the merchants' ships; she bringeth her food from afar. She riseth also while it is yet night, and giveth meat to her household, and a portion to her maidens.*

Many godly women have been up before anyone else, guiding the home, making sure that everything is fine. My darling grandmother had thirteen children. All kinds of grandchildren and other family members were packed in her house. I doubt if my grandparents knew who was in the house when they woke up in the morning. Before anyone else woke up, my grandmother had been up firing an old wood stove, getting breakfast ready.

The Bible says, *"She riseth also while it is yet night, and giveth meat to her household."* She realized that her great area of service and influence was her home. I know some women who must work outside the home and are under such pressure. My mother reared four children and tried to do the best she could. She had to work all her life.

There was a time when my wife worked outside the home, and it may come again. Just because you work outside the home does not mean you cannot make the home your priority. The home is to be your first place of importance and influence. You may need a little more help than some people need, but the virtuous woman puts her home where it should be.

The Word of God continues in verses sixteen through twenty-eight,

> *She considereth a field, and buyeth it: with the fruit of her hands she planteth a vineyard. She girdeth her loins with strength, and strengtheneth her arms. She perceiveth that her merchandise is good: her candle goeth not out by night. She layeth her hands to the spindle, and her hands hold the distaff. She stretcheth out her hand to the poor; yea, she reacheth forth her hands to the needy. She is not afraid of the snow for her household: for all her household are clothed with scarlet. She maketh herself coverings of tapestry; her clothing is silk and purple. Her husband is known in the gates, when he sitteth among the elders of the land. She maketh fine linen, and selleth it; and delivereth girdles unto the merchant. Strength and honour are her clothing; and she shall rejoice in time to come. She openeth her mouth with wisdom; and in her tongue is the law of kindness. She looketh well to the ways of her household, and eateth not the bread of idleness. Her children arise up, and call her blessed.*

I shall never forget boarding a plane after being told by a doctor that my mother was going to undergo an operation for a certain type of cancer and that, in his opinion, she only had a short time to live. During that trip, I took out a legal pad and began writing. I started with memories of my boyhood. I wrote down the stories of my mother taking me around in a little red wagon when she and I were alone together. I wrote down the stories of my mother going to work early in the morning. She would come into my room and whisper to me, "It's time to get up, I'm leaving. You make sure the others are up. There's breakfast on the table. I'm going to work, and I'll see you when you get home from school. Come by and see me on your way home, and let me know that everyone is safe."

When I wrote all those things down, I started thinking, "She's blessed. Her children rise up and call her blessed." Tell me, Mother, what do you want? What do you want from life? Would you like to have a better house, drive a safer car, wear nicer clothes? I hope you get all those things, but I believe more than all that, you would like to hear your children say, "I thank God for the kind of mother I had." Is that not better than all the other things combined?

> *We need virtuous mothers who will teach their sons to look for the right thing in the women they are going to marry, and that is a heart of virtue.*

"Her children arise up, and call her blessed." Do you know why? It is because she made her husband and her home, as far as earthly things are concerned, her priority. Her priority was not social concerns, or how important she was in the garden club, or how many people knew her at the parties; it was that her children and her husband knew she put them first. Because of the Lord Jesus, she put her home first.

There is something beautiful about that, and we have gotten away from it. If we do not tell our children this, who is going to tell them? The world, television, and movies are telling them just exactly the opposite of God's Word. Who is going to tell them the truth?

Ladies, desire in your heart to be a virtuous woman. You will be a crown to your husband. You will be the praise of your home. The Bible says, *"Her children arise up, and call her blessed; her husband also, and he praiseth her."* By the way, husbands, we do not praise our wives enough. I have been at too many funerals where husbands have said, "Pastor, I just didn't know what I had. I just didn't tell her." We should do a better job of praising her.

The Bible says in Proverbs 31:29-31,

> *Many daughters have done virtuously, but thou excellest them all. Favour is deceitful, and beauty is vain: but a woman that feareth the* LORD, *she shall be praised. Give her of the fruit of her hands; and let her own works praise her in the gates.*

In New Jersey, we lived in a beautiful old house in a fading Jewish community. My wife and I remodeled the whole thing; every room, every wall. There were some beautiful solid brass fixtures in the house. My wife polished the brass to make the fixtures look nice.

When we moved to Tennessee, we bought a house. There were also brass fixtures in the house we bought. My wife, God bless her, thought they were just like the ones in the house in New Jersey. She took some brass polish, and she

> *Ladies, desire in your heart to be a virtuous woman. You will be a crown to your husband.*

began polishing them. She found that they were not really solid brass; they only had an outer coat of brass. After some strong cleaning, all the brass color was gone. They looked like plumbing pipes! I came home, and she told me that she had cleaned the shine right off the fixtures. It was gone.

If all you are looking for in a person is the shine, you will find that the shine may not be very deep. If that is all you are looking for, you may look someday, and the shine could be gone. If you have solid brass through and through, the shine will never fade. The Bible says, *"Favour is deceitful, and beauty is vain."*

There is a beauty of the heart that makes a man grateful to say, "That is my wife." Children can fuss and get aggravated because you tell them no, but one of these days they will grow up. If their mother has lived a godly life, I will guarantee you, they will say, "I praise God for my mother." *"Who can find a virtuous woman?"*

Home Work

♦ Be the kind of wife your husband can trust.

♦ Have the beauty of the Lord on your life by spending time with Jesus Christ each day.

♦ Make your home your priority.

♦ See the home as your great place of service and influence for God.

♦ Place your husband and home first in importance above all other earthly concerns.

♦ Live such a godly life that your children will call you "blessed."

"For after this manner in the old time the holy women also, who trusted in God, adorned themselves, being in subjection unto their own husbands."

I Peter 3:5

Chapter Nine

Holy Women

 e think often of the holy men in the Bible, as in II Kings chapter four, where the Shunammite woman spoke of the prophet Elisha as the *"holy man"* of God. But the Bible also speaks of women who are *"holy women."* God's Word says in I Peter 3:5, *"For after this manner in the old time the holy women also, who trusted in God, adorned themselves, being in subjection unto their own husbands."*

In I Peter 1:15 the Bible says, *"But as he which hath called you is holy, so be ye holy in all manner of conversation; because it is written, Be ye holy; for I am holy."*

The Bible says in Deuteronomy 7:6, *"For thou art an holy people unto the LORD thy God: the LORD thy God hath chosen thee to be a special people unto himself, above all people that*

are upon the face of the earth." The Bible says God's people are to be a holy people, a chosen people, a special people above all people that are on the face of the earth.

In this perverse world, people should be able to look at a Christian woman and say, "She is a holy woman." There should be a distinct difference in the Christian woman. All around us we see the need for holy women.

We may be accused of meddling in matters that are not our business when we speak so plainly about such things, but remember, this is the Bible. These things not only *need* to be emphasized; they *must* be emphasized. We are living in a world that is swaying back and forth, without direction, aimlessly drifting, and this matter of holiness is absolutely essential.

THE MASTER OF THE HOLY WOMAN

The holy woman has a Master, the Lord Jesus Christ. In I Peter 3:1 the very first word is *"Likewise."* This, of course, is referring to something preceding. The reference is to the Lord Jesus Christ. In I Peter 2:21-25 the Bible says,

> *For even hereunto were ye called: because Christ also suffered for us, leaving us an example, that ye should follow his steps: who did no sin, neither was guile found in his mouth: who, when he was reviled, reviled not again; when he suffered, he threatened not; but committed himself to him that judgeth righteously: who his own self bare our sins in his own body on the tree, that we, being dead to sins, should live unto righteousness: by whose stripes ye were healed. For ye were as sheep*

*going astray; but are now returned unto the
Shepherd and Bishop of your souls.*

The Lord Jesus Christ is co-equal with God the Father and
God the Holy Spirit, yet He willingly humbled Himself, taking
a place of submission. The wife has no less value than the
husband, but the wife is to be like Christ, in humble submission
to her husband's leadership.

Christ left us an example of submitting Himself; He willingly
suffered for us. The Bible says in I Peter 3:1, *"Likewise, ye
wives, be in subjection to your own
husbands; that, if any obey not the
word, they also may without the
word be won by the conversation of
the wives."* The example the Lord
gives for the submission of the wife
to her husband is none other than
the Lord Jesus Christ.

This verse deals with the wife
who is a Christian and is married to
a man who is not a Christian. She is
not to divorce that man, leave that
man, or forsake that man; she is to
try to win that man to Christ. The
Bible says she can win him to Christ
by submitting to his authority and
living the Christian life day by day,

> *We are living in
> a world that is
> swaying back
> and forth,
> without
> direction,
> aimlessly
> drifting, and
> this matter of
> holiness is
> absolutely
> essential.*

giving the witness of her faith by her submissive attitude. This
is a powerful way of witnessing to her husband who is not
saved. She can win him to the Lord by living a life that testifies
that the gospel message is true.

No one is saved without the Word of God, and all of us
should do what we can to speak to people about the gospel. The
Bible explains that the wife can say what she wants, but if her

life does not back up her words, she is not going to win her husband to Christ.

After many years in the ministry, I have seen that most Christian women who are married to unsaved men do exactly the opposite of what the Bible teaches. They nag at their husbands night and day, belittling them, and talking to other people about what they do not do. If a woman does this, she is making her husband come to the place where he is ashamed to show his face around other Christians because he has been criticized in public in a way that should never have been done. This is not the instruction given in Scripture.

> *The example the Lord gives for the submission of the wife to her husband is none other than the Lord Jesus Christ.*

The holy woman has a Master. She realizes that her Master is Christ, and she allows her husband to be lord over her in the human relationship. She places herself in submission to her husband.

Submission is a dirty word to some people, but Christ has left us an example of submission. The holy woman submits herself; she places herself in subjection to her husband. She does not try to lead him; rather, she allows him to be the leader in the home.

We must understand that God's Word is not teaching that the husband is more valuable to God than the wife. Submission is not for value; it is for unity and for function in the home. There is one head in the home. It is very hard for all of us not to be manipulative. We plan, scheme, and connive trying to get something done some way other than God's way. This is not the way the holy woman lives.

If you are not submissive to your husband and your home is blessed with children, your children will learn rebellion from your lack of submission to your husband. The rebellion they learn from your lack of submission becomes an even greater hurt later in life as they become adults having never learned their place in marriage. In the case where men do not lead, their sons fail to learn how they are to lead their families.

> *If you are not submissive to your husband and your home is blessed with children, your children will learn rebellion from your lack of submission to your husband.*

If we could dissect our society and take a long, hard look at the source of our problems as a nation, we would conclude that the problem is in the home. Our homes need holy women who know the Lord, trust in the Lord, and are submissive to their husbands.

THE MANNER OF LIFE FOR THE HOLY WOMAN

There is a distinction in the life the holy woman lives. She does not pattern her life after the world. The Bible speaks very plainly about this in I Peter 3:2, *"While they behold your chaste conversation coupled with fear."* The word *"conversation"* has to do with our manner of life. This involves much more than what we say.

The Bible says that the holy woman's *"chaste conversation"* or chaste manner of life is coupled with fear. Notice the word *"fear"* in verse two. Notice also in verse six that God says not to be afraid. We are to fear God and not fear men. As we fear God and do not fear men, we find a great calm in life.

The word *"chaste"* means "to be free of that which is lewd." It means to have a pure thought life and seek to live a pure life. There is much lewdness in our world today. I am appalled at what people are willing to wear outside the home. I am appalled at the way many women dress to go shopping. It is far removed from a *"chaste"* manner of life. I am well aware that our apparel does not make us spiritual, but I am also aware that our apparel is a reflection of our spirituality.

We can improve our testimony for Christ by giving more thought to our behavior as Christians. Of course, our Christian life must be lived at its best in our home. If you are a holy woman, the way you behave outside your home will not betray the holy life.

The Bible says the holy woman's manner of life is *"coupled with fear."* This is a fear of God. I Peter 3:3 says, *"Whose adorning let it not be that outward adorning of plaiting the hair, and of wearing of gold, or of putting on of apparel."* It is interesting that God talks about *"chaste conversation,"* then He begins to explain that it is not the outward life that should get the emphasis, but the inward life.

All of us are apt to take this so far that we are proud of ourselves for the way we look. The Lord declares that we should have a chaste manner of life, but the emphasis is not on the outward appearance. The emphasis is on the hidden man walking with God. The Bible says in I Peter 3:3-4,

> *Whose adorning let it not be that outward adorning of plaiting the hair, and of wearing of gold, or of putting on of apparel; but let it be the hidden man of the heart, in that which is not*

*corruptible, even the ornament of a meek and quiet
spirit, which is in the sight of God of great price.*

Certain people leave no doubt that they love Jesus Christ. The beauty of the Lord is upon them. The Bible says holy women are to have a meek and quiet spirit. They are to be submissive and yielded to God. So many women are leading and loud, not meek and quiet. This is the spirit of our age.

Many young ladies, even teenage girls, are so loud and boisterous. They want to run everyone's business. There is nothing meek or quiet about them. This leaves little doubt as to what kind of women they will become.

There is something beautiful about this meekness and quietness. This is not weakness; it is meekness. Meekness is strength yielded to Christ. The Bible says, *"Which is in the sight of God of great price."*

In Ephesians 2:8-9 God's Word says, *"For by grace are ye saved through faith; and that not of yourselves: it is the gift of God: not of works, lest any man should boast."* Nothing we do merits salvation. Jesus Christ did all the work on the cross when He bled and died for our sins. We come to know Him as our Savior by asking Him to forgive our sin and by faith receiving Him as our Savior. Our salvation is not of works, lest any man should boast. Living a holy life gives evidence of salvation.

The way we dress has nothing to do with getting saved. The way we speak has nothing to do with getting saved. God's Word says that our salvation is *"not of works."* But let us not forget the very next verse in Ephesians 2:10, *"For we are his workmanship, created in Christ Jesus unto good works, which God hath before ordained that we should walk in them."* Our lives exemplify the workmanship of Jesus Christ. There was a day when Christian parents were more concerned about living holy lives and teaching their children to live holy lives for God.

Do I expect to change the world? No, I do not. But I do desire to strengthen the things that remain among the people of God.

The apostle Paul wrote to Timothy in I Timothy 2:9-10,

> *In like manner also, that women adorn themselves in modest apparel, with shamefacedness and sobriety; not with broided hair, or gold, or pearls, or costly array; but (which becometh women professing godliness) with good works.*

God's Word places the emphasis on the hidden man, not on the outward appearance. But the Bible also says that the outward appearance should be modest. Remember that every personal standard in the Christian's life should come out of a desire to live a holy life.

This is not weakness; it is meekness. Meekness is strength yielded to Christ. The Bible says, "Which is in the sight of God of great price."

Think about how much time we all spend in front of the mirror. Compare that to how much time we spend on our knees. Think of how much time we spend pampering ourselves and then how little attention we give to the way our hearts appear before God. We must place the emphasis where God places the emphasis. He places the emphasis on holiness and living a holy life.

Talk to your daughters about the way they look and how they appear to people. Teach them that they do not have to look a certain way to get a man. If they love Jesus Christ, someone who loves the Lord Jesus will love them for loving Christ. So many have confused sexuality with being attractive. The beautiful attraction

of a Christian's life comes from Christlikeness, not from any outward display of the body.

My heart hurts as I think of people that I know who started with a physical relationship and never got beyond that. They will never find the joy of the Lord. They will never know the peace and the oneness that God gives in a marriage union—oneness in spirit, oneness in soul, then oneness in body.

> *Do I expect to change the world? No, I do not. But I do desire to strengthen the things that remain among the people of God.*

Someone has said it is "sex o'clock" in America. It is not unusual to hear children talking about how they despise their bodies and hate the way they look. Many Christian families are as guilty as the rest of the world. There should be a different standard of living between people who know the Lord Jesus and people who do not know the Lord.

THE MINISTRY OF THE HOLY WOMAN

The holy woman has a great ministry. In I Peter 3:6, the example of Sara is used. She obeyed Abraham. She is referred to as a woman of *"old time"* and I might say of all time—a holy woman. Her ministry is an example for others to follow. The Lord lifts her up by saying, "Here is a woman that exemplifies what I am talking about."

How will the unsaved, biblically illiterate people who have heard nothing but the philosophy of the world, know how they are to conduct themselves? How will they ever know how to rear their children? They will learn these things only through the lives of holy women. This is the ministry of the holy woman.

Ladies, your first ministry is unto the Lord. In Mark 15:40-41 the Bible says,

> There were also women looking on afar off: among whom was Mary Magdalene, and Mary the mother of James the less and of Joses, and Salome; (who also, when he was in Galilee, followed him, and ministered unto him;) and many other women which came up with him unto Jerusalem.

Do you ever think of ministering to the Lord Jesus? The ministry of the holy woman is serving the Lord. Consider with me what the Bible says in Luke 8:1-3,

> And it came to pass afterward, that he went throughout every city and village, preaching and shewing the glad tidings of the kingdom of God: and the twelve were with him, and certain women...

Normally, we think of men serving the Lord, but look closely at the Scriptures.

> And certain women, which had been healed of evil spirits and infirmities, Mary called Magdalene, out of whom went seven devils, and Joanna the wife of Chuza Herod's steward, and Susanna, and many others, which ministered unto him of their substance.

The holy woman has a ministry unto the Lord Jesus. She also has a ministry to her husband. In the verse following this passage about women in I Peter chapter three, we find that the husband is to regard his wife in such a way that he gives honor to her. He considers her an heir, not someone he lords over but one who is equal with him in God's family. They are related in

the Lord. He realizes that if he is not right with his wife and she is not right with him, their prayers are hindered.

The wife should minister to the Lord, her husband, and to her children. God's greatest preachers are *"holy women"* who set a godly example for their children. Little girls and boys need to learn about holy living at their mother's knee. The father is to lead the home, but the mother is to guide the home, and the children are to learn from her. The Bible says in I Timothy 5:14, *"I will therefore that the younger women marry, bear children, guide the house, give none occasion to the adversary to speak reproachfully."*

> *We must place the emphasis where God places the emphasis. He places the emphasis on holiness and living a holy life.*

Mothers, be sure that your children know that their mother loves God and follows the clear commands of Scripture. Teach your little boys to be men and your little girls to be ladies. If you have a son, do not effeminize him. Little boys do not need to wear earrings and be adorned like little girls. God intends for them to grow up to be men. Little five-year-old girls do not need to be dressed as if they were teenagers. Often little girls are seen in public exposing parts of their bodies that should not be exposed. They soon lose their ability to blush and eventually have no shame. Holy women have a ministry to their children and should realize that sexual identity and modesty are absolutely essential.

Holy women also minister to other women. Every woman, no matter what age she may be, has a ministry to other women.

You may say, "I'm only eighteen years old." You have twelve-year-old girls who are looking up to you as an eighteen-year-old. You can minister to them by living a holy life.

You may say, "I'm only a twenty-three-year-old wife and mother." You have eighteen-year-old girls who are considering who they are going to marry. You can minister to them by living a holy life.

You may say, "I'm thirty-five or forty years old." There are twenty-five-year-old ladies who are married and starting a family, and they are wondering what they should emphasize and how they should live. You can minister to them by living a holy life.

You may say, "I'm a grandmother. I'm sixty-five years old." You have a ministry to the forty-five-year-old woman who is about to enter a different stage in life. No matter what stage of life you are in, you can have a ministry to other women simply by living a holy life.

It is disgusting to see so many women up in years trying to be sixteen years old again. Accept and enjoy each stage in life. God makes each season satisfying in Him. Do not live by the world's standards. The prime of life is any time in life that we are living in the center of the will of God. The holy woman has a ministry to other ladies.

The Bible says in Titus 2:3-5,

> *The aged women likewise, that they be in behaviour as becometh holiness, not false accusers, not given to much wine, teachers of good things; that they may teach the young women to be sober, to love their husbands, to love their children, to be discreet, chaste, keepers at home, good, obedient to their own husbands, that the word of God be not blasphemed.*

The Bible says the aged women are to teach the young women. If we ever cease to have the aged women in our churches living holy lives, then we are going to have a serious problem with the young women having no examples to follow.

Some of you with gray hair, who do not have the spring in your step you once had, have your greatest ministry ever. God has made life so that, as you grow older, your influence intensifies and enlarges. The statements you make now may have more impact on people's lives than at any other time.

The holy woman must have a master. She must be willing to submit herself to the Lord and to her husband. The holy woman's manner of life must be chaste, coupled with fear, and exemplified by a meek and quiet spirit. The holy woman's ministry is to the Lord, to her husband, to her children, and to other women.

On a flight to Europe, I was introduced to a missionary couple in their eighties. As I talked to the man, he was telling me of his ministry and how God had worked in his life. Seated beside him was his beautiful wife. They had been on the mission field for fifty years.

As I listened to the man and looked at his wife, she took such delight in what he was saying to me. Every hair in her head was white. To

> *Accept and enjoy each stage in life. God makes each season satisfying in Him. Do not live by the world's standards. The prime of life is any time in life that we are living in the center of the will of God.*

my knowledge, there was not a bit of makeup on her face, but she was so beautiful. Her smile was radiant. There was something grand and glorious in her countenance. The beauty of the Lord was upon her. I realized that she was a holy woman.

Ladies, you do not have to wait until your hair is white and you have been serving the Lord for fifty years to be a holy woman. You can be a holy woman in any stage of life when you are willing to seek the Lord and give Him the proper place in your life.

May God help us to receive this special emphasis deep into our hearts. Be a holy woman. The holy woman lifts the level of all those whom her life touches.

Home Work

- ♦ *Submit to the leadership of your husband just as Christ submitted to the Father.*

- ♦ *Do not pattern your life after the world.*

- ♦ *Have a pure thought life and seek to live a pure life.*

- ♦ *Dress in such a way that people have no doubt that you love Jesus Christ.*

- ♦ *Have a meek and quiet spirit.*

- ♦ *Place emphasis on the hidden man, not the outward appearance.*

- ♦ *Teach your children to live holy lives for God.*

- ♦ *Be an example for younger women to follow.*

"And she was in bitterness of soul, and prayed unto the LORD, and wept sore. And she vowed a vow, and said, O LORD of hosts, if thou wilt indeed look on the affliction of thine handmaid, and remember me, and not forget thine handmaid, but wilt give unto thine handmaid a man child, then I will give him unto the LORD all the days of his life, and there shall no razor come upon his head."

I Samuel 1:10-11

Chapter Ten

What Does It Mean to Give Your Child to God?

T his year in America, approximately six million children will be born. Very few of them will actually grow up in Christian homes, and only a small percentage of those in Christian homes will be given to God.

Giving a child to God means desiring what the Lord desires for that child. Letting go of children is a difficult thing, but in order to give our children to God, we must take our hands off and turn them loose for God's will and purpose. This is to continue all their lives as we sincerely believe that God's will is best for our children.

I am a husband and a father of two sons. Both sons are now married and have children of their own. I remember when they were born, and I remember all the hopes and dreams that I held

in my heart for them. I thank God for the privilege of seeing them grow up; I am an eyewitness of God's working in their lives. The Lord has taken care of them through many dangers. God has delivered and watched over them through these years.

> *Giving a child to God means desiring what the Lord desires for that child.*

Their mother and I, on our knees, gave both of our sons to God. I remember when we took them forward publicly in the house of God; we held them in our arms and presented them to the Lord. This was something we had already done privately. We gave them to the Lord. This was only the beginning of yielding them to the Lord for His plan and purpose.

In the opening chapter of I Samuel, we find the story of Elkanah and Hannah, the father and mother of Samuel. Many Christians know the story of Samuel and how God used him in such a marvelous way, a way unequaled by other men in his generation. God used him at a critical time in the history of the nation of Israel. All of this was the result of one woman's prayer. She asked God to give her a child, and she made a covenant with God that she would give that child back to Him.

As we think of the ills of our nation and the need for a Christ-honoring spiritual awakening, we need to remember how the Lord used the child that was given to Him and how the nation of Israel was blessed by the life of Samuel. May the Lord help us to give our sons and daughters to Him for His use.

The Lord records the beautiful story of Samuel and Hannah in I Samuel 1:10-11.

> *And she was in bitterness of soul, and prayed unto the LORD, and wept sore. And she vowed a vow, and said, O LORD of hosts, if thou wilt*

indeed look on the affliction of thine handmaid, and remember me, and not forget thine handmaid, but wilt give unto thine handmaid a man child, then I will give him unto the LORD all the days of his life, and there shall no razor come upon his head.

Hannah presented her son to God, but not just as a baby. Every day that he lived, she renewed the covenant she had made with the Lord. We must remember that yielding our children to God is not over when we present them to the Lord as newborns. This is only the beginning.

As she took him to the man of God, the Bible says in verses twenty-seven and twenty-eight of the same chapter,

> *Hannah presented her son to God, but not just as a baby. Every day that he lived, she renewed the covenant she had made with the Lord.*

For this child I prayed; and the LORD hath given me my petition which I asked of him: therefore also I have lent him to the LORD; as long as he liveth he shall be lent to the LORD. And he worshipped the LORD there.

In verse eleven, Hannah made her covenant with God. She said, *"I will give him unto the LORD all the days of his life."*

CHILDREN ARE A GIFT FROM GOD

We must realize that children are a gift from God. The Bible says in Psalm 127:1-3,

> *Except the LORD build the house, they labour in vain that build it: except the LORD keep the city, the watchman waketh but in vain. It is vain for you to rise up early, to sit up late, to eat the bread of sorrows: for so he giveth his beloved sleep. Lo, children are an heritage of the LORD: and the fruit of the womb is his reward.*

> *Letting go of children is a difficult thing, but in order to give our children to God, we must take our hands off and turn them loose for God's will and purpose.*

In this generation, there are children who have been labeled "throw-away kids." This phrase represents the godless ideas that have now become institutionalized in our world. We must be reminded over and over that children are a gift from God. The Bible says, *"Children are an heritage of the LORD."*

When conception takes place and life begins, it is a miraculous work of God. Children are a gift from the Lord.

In the thirty-third chapter of Genesis, we find the testimony of Jacob's reunion with Esau after being separated for quite a long time. Jacob was frightened about what would happen when he saw his brother Esau. The very tender story of their reunion is recorded in Genesis 33:4-5.

> *And Esau ran to meet him, and embraced him, and fell on his neck, and kissed him: and they*

wept. And he lifted up his eyes, and saw the women and the children; and said, Who are those with thee? And he said, The children which God hath graciously given thy servant.

Esau wanted to know who the people were. Jacob answered him, *"The children which God hath graciously given thy servant."* When you look at your children, are you reminded that they are the children God has given to you? Children are a gift from God.

CHILDREN ARE NOT OURS TO KEEP

Of course, we feel very possessive of our children. This is a natural instinct that God puts into the heart of a parent. Parents have a caring, loving feeling that is quite natural and necessary, but we must remember that we are not rearing them for ourselves. We are rearing them for Christ and for the mates they will meet and marry someday.

They are ours, but they are only ours to rear. They are placed into our care and keeping only for a while, although we continue the parent-child relationship throughout the years.

As we rear them, we are to keep in mind that what we must want for their lives is not our will but God's will. We must not try to conform them to our image; we must yield ourselves to God, praying that He will lead and direct our children, making them what He wants them to be. His desire is to transform them by the indwelling Holy Spirit into the likeness of Jesus Christ.

The most difficult thing for parents is trusting God with their children. But we must remember that we are rearing them for the Lord.

CHILDREN ARE TO BE GIVEN BACK TO GOD

Not only does the Bible teach us that children are given to us to rear, but also that we are to give them back to God. This is a deliberate decision parents must make. It is a covenant between parents and God. This means, in one sense, that we are to take our hands off the circumstantial dealings of their lives and realize that God can work through all things for their good and His glory. When things look bad, God can still work good out of the bad. When it seems as if someone has been brought into their lives who is not the person we would have chosen, in some way God can take that and turn it around for His glory and their good.

> *We must remember that yielding our children to God is not over when we present them to the Lord as newborns. This is only the beginning.*

Please do not misunderstand. We should never violate any biblical principle in the rearing of our children. Neither should our children use the violation of any biblical principle to justify what they are doing with their lives.

I can never be certain what my children are going to do in the future. I have tried to be careful about bragging about what they would or would not do. I never know where God is going to send them or what God is going to do with them.

When my mother held me in her arms as a baby, she had no idea that I would someday be the pastor of a church and president of a college. This is what God has chosen to do with my life. I am happy with what God has chosen to do with my life. God made me and He knows what is best for me. The Lord has led me and directed my life.

The Bible says in Romans 8:28, *"And we know that all things work together for good to them that love God, to them who are the called according to his purpose."* Parents should give their children back to God and trust God to direct their lives.

In the beautiful Bible story of Joseph, we find as Joseph revealed himself to his brethren that the Lord revealed Himself to Joseph in a wonderful way. Joseph recognized God's leading in his life. Joseph told his brethren that they had sold him but God had sent him (Genesis 45:5).

CHILDREN ARE TO LEARN ABOUT GOD IN THE HOME

The home is the natural place to learn about God and His ways. When asked if you have a Christian home, you might say, "I have a Bible in my home; I have plaques with Bible verses on the walls." But these things do not make a Christian home.

The fact that both parents are believers does not necessarily guarantee that the home is Christian. A Christian home is a home where Mom and Dad have yielded their lives to Christ. The Lord Jesus Christ is not simply a welcomed guest; He abides there. Not only are Christian books and Bibles found there, but it is also a place where the family members learn about God and what God wants them to do with their lives.

A Christian home is a home full of the love of Christ, a home where forgiveness is practiced and where people listen and care. It should be a natural place for instruction about the Lord and His work. This is what God desires. Having a Christian home has more to do with what we put into it than what we take out of it. Do not expect the church to be able to resurrect things of God that are put to death in your home.

INSTRUCTION BEGINS IN THE HEARTS OF THE PARENTS

Instruction must begin in the heart of the parent. The Bible says in Deuteronomy chapter six, verses four through six,

> *Hear, O Israel: The LORD our God is one LORD: and thou shalt love the LORD thy God with all thine heart, and with all thy soul, and with all thy might. And these words, which I command thee this day, shall be in thine heart.*

Why is it that we foolishly expect our children to do more than we do? How can we expect our children to believe more strongly about the Bible than we believe? How can we expect our children to love the church more than we love the church? Instruction must begin in the heart of every mom and dad.

As a parent, my commitment, my dedication, and my consecration to Jesus Christ must come first. As He chooses, God can bless and use children who have never had the privilege of living in a Christian home, but the ideal standard is for children to have Christian parents who instruct them in the Lord.

Every mother and father should make sure that they are saved and should seek the salvation of their children. Be sure that you have asked God to forgive your sin and have by faith received the Lord Jesus Christ as your personal Savior. Make sure that your children have no doubt that you are saved. Share your testimony with them. Live in such a way that they see Jesus Christ in your life.

As a parent, if there are things in your life that you know would grieve you if they were present in the lives of your children, ask God to help you rid your life of those things. Very few times in our lives do we, as parents, come to the place where we say, "Lord, not my will, but Your will be done." If Christian parents desire to see this surrender in the lives of their children, it must first take place in their own hearts.

What wonderful faith in God was expressed in the life of Moses' mother. Think of the moment when she took her hand off the basket that held her precious son and gave him completely into the hands of God.

TEACH YOUR CHILDREN DILIGENTLY

The Word of God teaches that when we give our children to God, this does not stop at the altar of the church. We must teach them diligently. The Bible says in Deuteronomy 6:7, *"And thou shalt teach them diligently..."* The word *diligent* means "to give our whole-hearted attention to it, to make it a matter of utmost importance, to make certain that it is done." Farther along we read, *"...teach them diligently unto thy children, and shalt talk of them when thou sittest in thine house, and when thou walkest by the way, and when thou liest down, and when thou risest up."*

There are two important things to know about teaching our children. First, we must always remain delighted with the opportunity to teach them. Sometimes this is not easy to do. I have heard parents say, "I give up. My children never pay attention. I'm sick of trying to teach them." God will not bless that spirit.

The Bible says in Proverbs 3:12, *"For whom the LORD loveth he correcteth; even as a father the son in whom he delighteth."* Although our children do not always do what we ask them to do, we are to be delighted to have the opportunity to work with them. This is grounded in our understanding that God gave us our children. Could it be that in dealing with our children, God also speaks to us concerning things that need to receive attention in our own lives?

To teach our children diligently, we must always remember that we are to delight in the opportunity to work with them. This is the parent's responsibility. Many parents need to ask God to forgive them. They have given up on working with their children. They have forgotten to delight in this wonderful opportunity God has given them.

The second thing we must learn about teaching our children is that their hearts must remain receptive and teachable. The Bible says in Proverbs 1:7, *"The fear of the LORD is the beginning of knowledge: but fools despise wisdom and instruction."*

> *A Christian home is a home where Mom and Dad have yielded their lives to Christ. The Lord Jesus Christ is not simply a welcomed guest; He abides there.*

There is responsibility on the part of the parent and on the part of the child. The responsibility of the parent is to delight in the opportunity to instruct. The responsibility of the child is to be willing to be instructed.

Giving a child to God does not mean that we make a single decision, pray a single prayer, and our responsibility is fulfilled. To give a child to God means to realize that as He gives us these precious gifts, they are ours to rear for Him. There must be a deliberate decision to give them back to God.

The home is to be a place of natural instruction. The hearts of the parents must first be moved and touched with the things of God. Then, we must diligently teach our children, always delighting in the opportunity, and pray that our children will be receptive to the truths we teach them from God's Word.

We must be certain that our greatest joy is what God desires it to be. The Bible says in III John 4, *"I have no greater joy than to hear that my children walk in truth."*

What is to become of these children that God has given us? Our children should be a blessing, not a burden. This blessing comes from realizing that they were given to us by God.

There must be something that we desire for our children above all else. Someone may say, "I want my children to be healthy." Someone else may say, "I want my children to be athletic." Another says, "I want my children to sing." Some parent may say, "I want my children to have a nice house and a good job. I want them to have many wonderful things in life." You may want these things for your children, but there must be something at the top of the list.

> *There is responsibility on the part of the parent and on the part of the child. The responsibility of the parent is to delight in the opportunity to instruct. The responsibility of the child is to be willing to be instructed.*

When a young couple finds themselves in the hospital room with their newborn baby, they should pray, "Lord, Thou hast given us this child and we give this child back to Thee. Help us be responsible parents in rearing this child in the way Thou hast designed in Thy Word. Our earnest prayer and highest goal for this child is that this child lives and walks in Thy truth."

There are things that every father thinks his children should do and could do, but there is one thing that should be our greatest joy. No matter where they are or what they are doing as far as the world is concerned, one thing should thrill the heart of a Christian parent more than any other thing, and that is to see his children truly living the truth of God. *"I have no greater joy than to hear that my children walk in truth."*

To give a child to God means to realize that as He gives us these precious gifts, they are ours to rear for Him. There must be a deliberate decision to give them back to God.

What do you want for your children? When we give them to God, we are saying, "I want for them what God wants for them." His desire is for them to walk in truth.

Lead them to know Christ as their personal Savior. Be sensitive to the opportunities the Lord provides to speak to your children specifically about knowing Christ as Savior. Keep them in faithful attendance to a Bible-teaching, Bible-preaching church. Read God's Word with them daily. Help them to memorize God's Word. Teach them the great stories of the Bible. Pray with them and for them. Kneel beside them and allow them to lead in prayer. Hear them speak to God. As parents, live the truth of God before them each day.

Home Work

♦ Desire God's will, not your own will, for your children.

♦ Pray that God will lead your children and make them what He wants them to be.

♦ Make a deliberate decision to give your children back to God.

♦ Provide a Christian home where your children can receive instruction about God and His work.

♦ Be sure you have trusted Christ by faith as your Savior and seek the salvation of your children.

♦ Do not expect your children to be stronger Christians than you are willing to be.

♦ Diligently teach your children the Word of God.

♦ Read the Bible with your children every day and teach them the great stories of the Bible.

♦ Keep your children in faithful attendance to church.

♦ Desire for your children, above all else, that they walk in the truth.

"Remember now thy Creator in the days of thy youth, while the evil days come not, nor the years draw nigh, when thou shalt say, I have no pleasure in them."

Ecclesiastes 12:1

Chapter Eleven

Youth at Risk

 he book of Ecclesiastes is a beautiful book of the Bible but a neglected one. The preacher is Solomon, and he preaches a sermon about life. In this sermon he tells us that life under the sun without the Lord is vanity. Over thirty times in this one message he plunges deep into life and comes up with his hands empty.

He says that, as king, he could have anything his heart desired. He could get any woman he wanted. Anything that he wanted, he got. However, after having all that he wanted, he still found that life without God was empty.

Coming to the end of the sermon, he concludes the whole matter with the fact that we are to fear God and keep His commandments. In the first verse of chapter twelve he says, *"Remember now thy Creator in the days of thy youth, while the*

evil days come not, nor the years draw nigh, when thou shalt say, I have no pleasure in them."

"Youth at risk" is a term that is being tossed around a great deal today. The term has to do with sexual activity among young people and the idea of using preventative measures to avoid the HIV virus.

The posture being promoted by most seems very simple. Since kids cannot be stopped, some type of sexual contraceptives should be given to young people in junior high school and high school to keep them from getting AIDS.

> *The sexual relationship between a husband and wife is God's gift to marriage. Outside of marriage the sexual relationship is sin.*

I want to be as clear as I can be on this matter. This is not the biblical position. The biblical position is abstinence before marriage. There is no way to make anything else out of what the Bible teaches. The sexual relationship between a husband and wife is God's gift to marriage. Outside of marriage the sexual relationship is sin.

Many are resorting to other things because they have conceded that the battle for this generation of young people has already been lost. This battle for a generation of young people is not won or lost in the schools or even in the churches. The battleground is the home. As the home goes, so goes the nation.

There is no such thing as "safe sex." How many people do you know who have children that they did not plan to have? They did what they thought was necessary to keep from having those children, but it failed.

The risk to young people is not a sexual risk. There will come a day when young people who have not remembered God in their youth will have no pleasure in their lives. Consider the verse. *"Remember now thy Creator in the days of thy youth, while the evil days come not, nor the years draw nigh, when thou shalt say, I have no pleasure in them."*

The message here is very simple. We remember God in the days of our youth in order to enjoy all the days of our lives. We remember God in the days of our youth to get the full pleasure out of the days of our lives. It is common to find young people today, only eighteen or nineteen years old, who have already burned out on life. They have tried everything. They have done everything there is to do, but there is no pleasure to be found.

One so-called rock star said recently, "We have broken every rule and there is nothing left to do but start over and break any new ones we find."

I want to remind you that biblical values are not simply for one generation, they are for every generation. Proverbs 30:11-14 says,

> *There is a generation that curseth their father, and doth not bless their mother. There is a generation that are pure in their own eyes, and yet is not washed from their filthiness. There is a generation, O how lofty are their eyes! and their eyelids are lifted up. There is a generation, whose teeth are as swords, and their jaw teeth as knives, to devour the poor from off the earth, and the needy from among men.*

God's Word also says in Judges 2:8-10,

> *And Joshua, the son of Nun, the servant of the LORD, died, being an hundred and ten years old. And they buried him in the border of his inheritance in Timnathheres, in the mount of*

*Ephraim, on the north side of the hill Gaash.
And also all that generation were gathered unto
their fathers: and there arose another
generation after them, which knew not the LORD,
nor yet the works which he had done for Israel.*

The crisis in the world today is not a population explosion. It is not an environmental crisis. It is not a crisis of contagious diseases. The real crisis in the world today is that there is a generation that does not know the Lord, neither do they know the mighty works that God has done. The responsibility this brings to those of us who know Christ is staggering.

I remember talking to a pizza maker in a well-known pizza place. I wanted to know his secret to great pizza. I asked, "What makes your pizza so good?" He said, "One minute." I thought he was saying to me, "I'll tell you in one minute." But he said, "One minute." I said, "I beg your pardon?"

He said, "What makes our pizza so good is one minute. Do you notice how carefully we watch these ovens? There is only one minute between a good pizza and a bad pizza. We use the best ingredients, but in the cooking process, the pizza must be removed in that one minute. If it is before that minute or after that minute, it is no good."

God's "special minute" in life is *"the days of our youth."* Of course, people can be forgiven of awful things they have done and can be cleansed by the blood of Jesus Christ, but the time of our youth is the time to lay the foundation for all of life.

Youth are at risk. This is why we must work so hard. This is why we should give ourselves devotedly to what God has given us to do. This is why a pastor's heart must be a heart for the whole ministry. We must have a strong preschool program, from birth through the preschool years. We must have a strong children's program. We must also have a strong youth program.

To be strong means to be strong in the Lord, His Word, His grace, and strong in His love. The people who are doing all this work must be the adults in the church. Our great work is to help them. *"Remember now thy Creator in the days of thy youth."*

We witness each day the fruit of a generation that has forgotten God. Young people are at risk, but the great risk is not the AIDS virus; there are other risks that are far greater.

UNDERSTANDING SALVATION IS AT RISK

The word *risk* means "danger" or "peril." Young people are at risk because so much has been substituted for the clear gospel message. The gospel has never lost its power, but it needs messengers to proclaim it. It is still the power of God unto salvation, but so many are ashamed of it. When the message of salvation is at risk, it is in peril. We are facing a greater peril than the peril of the AIDS epidemic.

It is indescribably worse to die and go to hell than it is to have anything else happen in your life. We must make sure that we never tire or stray from the gospel message. The apostle Paul declared in I Corinthians 2:2, *"For I determined not to know anything among you, save Jesus Christ, and him crucified."*

We live in an increasingly secularized society. We must never be ashamed to preach the old truth of the Word of God, to give out the gospel, to tell the truth to people about heaven and hell. We must speak up and speak clearly to the youth of this generation.

While flying to a speaking engagement, I had an empty seat near me and a lady asked, "May I sit in that seat?" I said, "Certainly." When she took her place there in the same row with me, she started unpacking her things. She appeared to be a rather intelligent person. She put on her headphones and got out a great, big book that I recognized. She started listening to a tape through her headphones, took her marker out, and began marking through her big book.

When I saw that there was a break in her intensity, I wanted to witness to her about Christ. So I started a conversation. She said, "It is interesting that you should ask me about religion because I am reading a religious book." She was reading the primer on the New Age Movement by Marilyn Ferguson. It has to do with miracles. It is one of the books that is used to introduce people to the New Age Movement. The New Age Movement has a common denominator and that is the denial of the deity of Jesus Christ and His suffering for salvation.

> *Young people are at risk because so much has been substituted for the clear gospel message.*

She thought she was entering into some great religious experience, and she was. But it was a religion without Christ. That was not the worst of it. I said to her, "Where do you go to church?" She said she went to the Unitarian church. They do not believe in the Bible, in the God of the Bible, or in the Trinity. She said, "I'm not taking this study at my Unitarian church."

She was being very kind about it. She gave the name of a well-known Presbyterian church in our city, and she said, "That is where I am going each week for this study on the New Age Movement, to get into the religion of the New Age."

I know some Presbyterian churches in our town that preach the gospel and try to get people saved. But you cannot imagine the shock that went through my system when I heard that a Presbyterian church was the meeting place for people to discuss channels, demon possession, spirit guides, and other New Age beliefs.

People in this world are lost in sin, and they are going to die without Jesus Christ. As those people drive by a place that says "Church," they will go inside thinking they are going to hear the truth.

Understanding the way of salvation is in peril today. There is so much confusion about God and heaven and hell. May God help us to zealously keep giving the gospel and telling people how to be saved. May God also help those of us who know the Lord to be out winning people to Jesus Christ. There has never been a greater time for soul winners to be in the harvest field.

STANDARDS OF PERSONAL DECENCY ARE AT RISK

The importance of personal decency is in peril. God's people are to be a holy people. Sadly, the standards of the world have been taken as the standards for the children of God.

Our local paper recently reported the events of a pop rock group that came to town. The entire article was about one of the performers in the group. The young man had not reached his eighteenth birthday. I cannot even use the same terms that were in the article, but one caption by his picture flatly denied that he would stop pulling his pants off during his concerts.

The article went on to describe his concerts. They are attended, for the most part, by preteens. Children from the ages of nine through twelve made up most of the

> *The gospel has never lost its power, but it needs messengers to proclaim it. It is still the power of God unto salvation, but so many are ashamed of it.*

audience. These groups that appeal to preteen age children are ungodly. They say their aim is to introduce young people to a sexual experience.

> *Personal decency is in peril today. An entire generation is staggering through life in a maze of unbridled sexual activity.*

God's Word says that if you do not remember your Creator in the days of your youth, you will not have pleasure in your life, real pleasure, the enduring kind that only God can give.

The article says that during the concerts little nine, ten, and eleven-year-old girls take off their private clothes, throw them on stage, and call out filthy words. Personal decency is in peril today. An entire generation is staggering through life in a maze of unbridled sexual activity.

This behavior is not acceptable even if it is protected. What about the church? What about the home? God's children must raise a standard of decency for this decadent generation.

THE STABILITY OF THE CHRISTIAN FAMILY IS AT RISK

I grew up in a broken home. I know what that is like. I admire anyone who tries to put a broken home back together. I admire anyone who tries to get on with his life and make the most of what he has left. Many people have been helped, but there is no one in his right mind who would say he wants his home to break up.

The stability of the Christian family is at risk. You may be trying to build a strong family, but the Devil is trying to tear

your family down. The world, the flesh, and the Devil want your young people. They want your children. They want your husband. They want your wife. The home is under attack.

Let me recommend a reprint from the *Reader's Digest* entitled, "The Feminist Betrayal." Sally Quinn, the writer of this article, states:

> Our leaders, the people who spoke for the feminist movement were never completely honest. They were hypocritical. It is like the Communist who denied the existence of God and the right to worship; leaders of the feminist movement overlooked the deepest, most fundamental needs of their constituency.
>
> The leaders of the movement, though they never blinked, instead of helping women fulfill their needs, acted as if women had but one side and ignored the reality of husbands and children.

Quinn says the movement became an anti-male, anti-child, anti-family, and anti-feminine movement. After all of that she says, "It has nothing to do with us as women."

Quinn speaks of the leaders and says,

> 'You can do it all. Look at us.' This was the message they gave. Women who struggled to make it work and failed were often hurt more than helped by these phony examples of how wonderful life could be if they would only take charge and discard the men. Women felt ashamed to be housewives, ashamed to be full-time mothers.

We are not living in the forties, fifties, or the sixties; we are living in an age when women have been made to feel embarrassed for saying they are housewives or mothers.

There are some ladies who have to work outside the home. My darling mother had to work sometimes twelve or fourteen hours a day to rear a family. There are some families where moms and dads both have to work. But God forbid that we ever look down on someone because she is a "mother" or a "housewife." The family is under attack.

What kind of signal do you think we are sending to young people? What kind of pressure is this putting on young ladies who feel as if they have to go out and try to attain some powerful position or they will have no value at all?

The Christian family is the greatest institution on earth. It preserves the best things. It teaches things that no other institution on earth is commissioned to teach. Even a church cannot substitute for a Christian home. Parents need to say, "God, help me to dedicate my life to make my home what it should be."

> *You may be trying to build a strong family, but the Devil is trying to tear your family down.*

Young people today are hearing the church minimized. When you criticize what is being done in a Bible-believing, Bible-preaching church, you are destroying the lives of your young people. Someday they will need the pastor, but they will not listen to him. Someday they will need the Sunday School teacher, but they will not listen to him or her. Someday they will need what the message of the church can do for them, but they will not hear it.

Parents can say all they want to say about how good the church is, but when they sit at home or on the boat or in some mountain cabin on the Lord's Day, they are telling their children, "The church does not mean what it should mean to me." When you are not faithful to attend church, you are sending the wrong signal to your children.

> *The home is the basic institution on which this civilization was built.*

The home is the basic institution on which this civilization was built. But where is the help for our homes today? Where is the standard of righteousness raised?

Bring your children to the right church and in love and compassion, the pastor will stand behind what you are trying to do with your children. We are in this fight together. Hold your ground. The dating practices the world uses that allow girls to go anywhere, anytime, with anyone, are wrong. Your children may say, "Mother and Daddy, you are mistreating me because you have old-fashioned ways." Hold to your ways. If you bring them to the house of God, the faithful pastor is going to stand with you.

If you want them to look and behave like the rest of the world, then just turn them loose; but that is not what you want. Your pastor is in your corner trying to say, "God bless you, Mom and Dad, I am standing with you."

We need old-fashioned, Bible-believing, sin-hating churches today. We do not have enough of them. When a lady can sit in the same aisle with me on the airplane and say that the most devilish thing in the world is being taught in a church that is supposed to be teaching the truth, I say it is high time we wake up and declare that we do not have to apologize for taking a stand for what is right. Our homes are greatly helped by the right kind of church.

The risks we face are not imaginary—they are real! Let us stand the ground God has given us and press forward to greater heights for His glory and the good of this generation.

Home Work

♦ Stand strongly for abstinence before marriage because it is the biblical position.

♦ Give children and teenagers the clear gospel message of salvation.

♦ Uphold personal standards of decency and modesty.

♦ Follow the teaching of God's Word, not the standards of the world.

♦ Remember that a church cannot substitute for a Christian home.

♦ Bring your family to church faithfully, knowing that your home is greatly helped by a Bible-believing pastor and church.

"And these words, which I command thee this day, shall be in thine heart: and thou shalt teach them diligently unto thy children, and shalt talk of them when thou sittest in thine house, and when thou walkest by the way, and when thou liest down, and when thou risest up. And thou shalt bind them for a sign upon thine hand, and they shall be as frontlets between thine eyes. And thou shalt write them upon the posts of thy house, and on thy gates."

Deuteronomy 6:6-9

Chapter Twelve

Seizing the Golden Moments in Life

 ife has its golden moments. The oldest psalm in the book of Psalms, the ninetieth Psalm, speaks of a man living threescore and ten years. God's Word goes on to say, *"If by reason of strength they be fourscore years, yet is their strength labour and sorrow; for it is soon cut off, and we fly away."* We move swiftly through life, and the golden moments must be seized.

About the time that God gave Moses the ninetieth Psalm to pen, He also gave him the words in Deuteronomy 6:1-12. The Bible says in this passage,

> *Now these are the commandments, the statutes, and the judgments, which the LORD your God commanded to teach you, that ye might do them in the land whither ye go to*

possess it: that thou mightest fear the LORD thy God, to keep all his statutes and his commandments, which I command thee, thou, and thy son, and thy son's son, all the days of thy life; and that thy days may be prolonged. Hear therefore, O Israel, and observe to do it; that it may be well with thee, and that ye may increase mightily, as the LORD God of thy fathers hath promised thee, in the land that floweth with milk and honey. Hear, O Israel: The LORD our God is one LORD: and thou shalt love the LORD thy God with all thine heart, and with all thy soul, and with all thy might. And these words, which I command thee this day, shall be in thine heart: and thou shalt teach them diligently unto thy children, and shalt talk of them when thou sittest in thine house, and when thou walkest by the way, and when thou liest down, and when thou risest up. And thou shalt bind them for a sign upon thine hand, and they shall be as frontlets between thine eyes. And thou shalt write them upon the posts of thy house, and on thy gates. And it shall be, when the LORD thy God shall have brought thee into the land which he sware unto thy fathers, to Abraham, to Isaac, and to Jacob, to give thee great and goodly cities, which thou buildedst not, And houses full of all good things, which thou filledst not, and wells digged, which thou diggedst not, vineyards and olive trees, which thou plantedst not; when thou shalt have eaten and be full; Then beware lest thou forget the LORD, which brought thee forth out of the land of Egypt, from the house of bondage.

There is an amusing story of a teacher who came to her class on the first day of school and said, "I want all of you little children to know that I am an atheist, and I would like to know how many of you are atheists." In order to please the teacher, all the children except one raised their hands and said that they were atheists.

This singled out one little girl who would not raise her hand. So the teacher, in an attempt to embarrass the child said, "And may I ask, what are you?" The girl replied, "I'm a Christian." The teacher said, "Why are you a Christian?" The child answered, "I'm a Christian because my mommy and my daddy are Christians and they have told me about Christ and I'm a Christian."

The teacher said, "So you're a Christian because your mommy and daddy are Christians." The little girl replied, "That's right." To embarrass the child further, the teacher said, "What if your mommy and daddy were morons? What would you be?" The little girl said, "I'd be an atheist like you." She had it right.

We need the help of heaven in our homes. God wants us to take care of our homes. In this Bible passage from the book of Deuteronomy, we have an amazing scene, and in this scene there is a very amazing man. One of the great mountain peaks of Old Testament Scripture, the man Moses, stood to address all the people of God, charging them with God's commands.

The book of Deuteronomy is part of what is called the Pentateuch, the first five books of the Bible. Someone may say to you that the book of Deuteronomy is just a repetition of other things we find in Exodus, Leviticus, and Numbers. It is more than that. Never imagine that there is one redundant word in Scripture. God has a message for all of us in this book.

Moses spoke about the only true and living God. We live in a world with many gods. Many people think it is sufficient to simply have a god, any god. The only true and living God, God Eternal, God Almighty, Creator God is the God of the Bible who gave His Son, the Lord Jesus Christ, to die for our sin.

The Bible declares in Deuteronomy 6:2, *"That thou mightest fear the LORD thy God."* Verse three says, *"Hear therefore, O Israel, and observe to do it; that it may be well with thee."*

Can we wonder why so many things are not going well when obedience is the secret to God's blessing, and Christians are not obedient? So many Christians have knowledge but are not obedient to the knowledge they have. The secret to God's blessing is not knowledge, but obedience. God said we are to hear and do these things. He said, *"Hear therefore, O Israel."* Let us hear and heed God's Word.

Moses thundered forth as he spoke to the people, *"Hear, O Israel: The LORD our God is one LORD: and thou shalt love the LORD thy God with all thine heart, and with all thy soul, and with all thy might."* God is working in all our lives to bring us to the place where we love Him supremely.

Verse six says, *"And these words, which I command thee this day, shall be in thine heart."* If we do not have Him in our hearts, we cannot teach His Word to others. If you hear someone teaching and preaching from his head, his speech may be perfectly memorized and he may speak articulately and in a way that is winsome; but there is a great difference between speaking from the head and speaking from the heart. What we must deal with is the home, the family unit. It is possible to travel the world over, be acclaimed by many to be someone important, receive all kinds of awards, and think you have many friends, only to go home to an unhappy place and actually be a very unhappy person. Let us take care of our home life. We must seize the golden moments.

"And these words, which I command thee this day, shall be in thine heart: and thou shalt teach them diligently unto thy children." In other words, every generation must be responsible for teaching the truth of God to the next generation.

I had a pleasant childhood. If I were to tell you all the things that happened to me as a child, you might say, "How could you have had a pleasant childhood?" There is a certain way that children deal with things in order to find the joy and cheer in it all. My little playmates, my brother and two sisters, and my mother–who was so much like a little girl–often played together. I had a happy childhood, so much so that as I grew up and was separated from my family, I thought how much I missed childhood.

The truth is, we cannot remain children forever, and we cannot be playmates forever. God has designed life so that as we move through it, it is not to get worse; it is to get better and better. There are certain things, things of God and God's Word, that can be placed in the hearts and minds of children in the formative years of their lives that shape them into faithful friends and brothers and sisters and make them strong for life.

> *So many Christians have knowledge but are not obedient to the knowledge they have. The secret to God's blessing is not knowledge, but obedience. God said we are to hear and do these things.*

As we think about children not receiving these things, we question what kind of adults they are going to become. All grown men were once little boys running and playing, carefree and joyous. Those who received the right kind of moral lessons and decent instruction, the character-building things that came from knowing Christ and His Word, have grown into men who can be strong friends, faithful companions, the right kind of husbands, the right kind of fathers, and the right kind of grandfathers. Life does not get worse and worse; it gets better and better and stronger and stronger until someday we see the face of Jesus Christ. This is the way God intended for it to be.

> *It is possible to travel the world over, be acclaimed by many to be someone important, receive all kinds of awards, and think you have many friends, only to go home to an unhappy place and actually be a very unhappy person.*

All grown women were once little girls playing with dolls and imagining all kinds of things while having tea parties with playmates and friends. After passing through that stage in life, one could imagine that the joy was gone, the cheerfulness of life had vanished forever. But God does not intend for it to be this way. You cannot be little playmates forever. Life moves on, and people grow up and become adults.

When the right things are placed in childhood, in the formative years of life, those little girls can grow up to be the right kind of mothers and sisters and friends and grandmothers that are desperately needed in our world. This is why the home is so important. This is why we must seize the golden moments, because they do not last forever. These moments come quickly and must be seized by parents who intend to do the best they can do with the responsibilities of parenthood given to them by the Lord.

WHEN THOU SITTEST IN THINE HOUSE

God spells out these golden moments for us. Make note of them well. The Word of God says, *"When thou sittest in thine house."*

Most people do not have a home; they only have a hotel because the only thing they do in their house is sleep. All of us need an awakening about our homes, not our houses, but making our houses into the homes they should be. A house is a place; a home is people.

It is sad to become older and discover many things you should have known about the true values in life when you were much younger. Godly parents can help their children place the emphasis in life where it should be placed.

All adults have deep dies cast. Just as our brows are wrinkled, our minds are creased with thoughts and ideas. I thought recently about my experience with my precious mother when she was dying. I was lying in the bed beside her, stroking her forehead. As I think about it now, I can still feel the deep wrinkles in her brow. She developed those from rearing four children and, for the most part, doing it alone. I am comforted by the fact that the next time I see her, her face will be fresh with eternal youth. Just as she developed those wrinkles on her outward appearance, she developed through the years into a certain type of person. Home is to be the center for this development.

We need to reconsider the golden moments we have in our homes. How precious it is to have a meal together and have everyone there. It is precious to have children at home and have the opportunity to talk with them. It is precious to be able to sit down and share conversations about the goodness of God. He has given us language and we can communicate, not only with words, but also with feelings of love and commitment. We need to seize the golden moments that God gives us in our homes to speak for Christ and to honor God.

Every child should feel as if he is in the safest, sweetest, most joyous place on the face of the earth when he walks in the front door of his house. Mom and Dad must work at this. Mom and Dad have to make this happen. Mom and Dad have to diligently say, "We're going to do something for our children that will remain with them all the days of their lives. We're going to seize the golden moments that God gives us at home. We are going to work diligently at making our home the right kind of place."

> *There are certain things, things of God and God's Word, that can be placed in the hearts and minds of children in the formative years of their lives that shape them into faithful friends and brothers and sisters and make them strong for life.*

Hurry is the scourge of family life. We have more time-saving devices than any other generation that ever lived. Because of this, we attempt to do more in limited amounts of time than any other generation attempted to do. Because we attempt to do so many things in so little time, we are always rushed and we have time for no one, not even ourselves. Every one of us will look back some day with regret that we did not seize more of the golden moments we had when we were together in our homes. How precious it is to be able to talk to our children as we sit in our houses. This is truly a golden moment.

WHEN THOU WALKEST BY THE WAY

The second golden moment God gives us in life is *"when thou walkest by the way."* This particular expression is referring to responsibilities we must fulfill on a daily basis, duties God gives us in life. See in this more than duty, more than something that must be done "when we walk by the way."

When we are attending to something that has to be attended to "when we walk by the way," we must recognize it as a golden moment God has given us to share, especially with our children.

There are things that Mother will have to do on a daily basis with children, routine things that must be done, things that have to do with hygiene and cleanliness. These are not simply activities. These are specific things that provide golden moments for us to touch our children and say things to them, speaking in such a way that they will never forget how precious life is and how good God is. This is a golden moment.

> *Godly parents can help their children place the emphasis in life where it should be placed.*

It is sweet to see a daughter making cookies with her mother and sharing them with her daddy. It is pleasant to see a little boy helping his daddy do something. Though at first he may appear to be an annoyance because he is in the way, do not let his help be a bother. This is a golden moment God gives you to have your son by your side. His hands may not be quite as nimble as yours and his coordination may not be quite as developed as yours is, but you have moments to share with him in an activity, in a duty. This responsibility, doing something that has to be done, becomes a loving, teaching time.

This is a time to share things together about the Lord and His goodness. It is a golden moment!

WHEN THOU LIEST DOWN

The third golden moment God gives us is *"when thou liest down."* So many miss this moment. Sleep is such a beautiful, wonderful gift from God.

Make special note of Psalm 4:8. The Bible says, *"I will both lay me down in peace, and sleep: for thou, LORD, only makest me dwell in safety."* You never know how much sleep means until you cannot sleep. You do not know what a good night's rest means until you cannot get one. Due to a serious spine condition, I went for two years without a good night's rest. I thank the Lord for the successful surgery that He allowed me to have that corrected this problem.

God says, "I'm going to give you a golden moment with your children. It is when they lie down to sleep." There should be no arguing, harsh words, or loudness at bedtime. Mom and Dad should never be engaged in heavy conversation when it is time for children to be put to bed. This golden moment God gives you at their bedside each evening is something never to be forgotten. It is not just for that moment, it is a part of life that is placed into the character of that human being. It is woven into that life and is going to make a better mother, a better father, a better brother, a better sister, a better friend, or a more faithful companion of that person. In most houses, the children go to bed when they want to go to bed. They do as they please. What golden moments are missed!

As much as possible, everything in the house should come to a halt when it is time for children to go to bed. The television should be off. Things should be put aside. This is a precious, golden moment. At bedtime, there should be a calm in the house. There should be a sweet peace. There should be a precious feeling in the air that cannot be defined but certainly can be felt.

As much as possible, Mom and Dad should kneel beside the bed. The spiritual responsibility of putting children to bed should not be assigned to Mother all the time when there is a father in the house. A beautiful bedtime story from the Bible should be read. A sweet, calming peace can be given because of faith in God. Little minds that are troubled and wearied with things they have heard during the day should be put to rest. Sweet thoughts of God and His goodness and His care and keeping of their lives should be on their minds as they go to sleep.

This golden moment God gives you at their bedside each evening is something never to be forgotten.

The golden moment of bedtime can be seized for God and God's glory. It is not only important to do this for children, it is important for parents to do this. Make a habit of never getting into any argument with your children just before going to bed. Do not read anything that is terribly disturbing before going to bed. Do not look through news magazines before going to bed. If you read, read something that is peaceful and sweet. Everyone needs rest, and God wants to calm our troubled lives. God's Word says, *"Man that is born of a woman is of few days, and full of trouble"* (Job 14:1). There is a golden moment to be seized, and it is bedtime. Ask God to give you the wisdom to seize this golden moment.

WHEN THOU RISEST UP

The fourth golden moment is *"when thou risest up."* Starting the day is a golden moment. Having the right attitude when we rise from sleep has so much to do, not just with the day, but with life, because life is made of days. The right attitude is the attitude of gratitude and pleasantness. Parents should not scream at their children, "Get out of bed! You're going to be late for school!"

A parent may say, "I have to scream like that." No, you do not. Stop teaching your children that they must be screamed at and scolded in order to do things. Express the right kind of authority as a parent in your home and calmly take control.

Think of the dividends of a happy, joyous, wonderful home life where parents have fulfilled their responsibility and have seized the golden moments in life.

If you have trained your children in such a way that they must be told ten or fifteen times to do something, then they have never taken you seriously enough as a parent. Because there is increasing failure in the home, it staggers my mind to think about what we are going to face in the future.

Children should be greeted pleasantly. On the night before, preparations can be made for the next morning. The day does not have to begin like a treasure hunt, trying to find where a shoe, a sock, a pair of pants, or a shirt is. All these things can be found the evening before, so that it is not a part of the confusion of the day. Prepare in the evening for the following day.

There should be a pleasant time with the family when God's Word is read, when prayers are offered to the Lord. There should be a time to rise. Be up early enough not to be rushed. When you are rushed, one person gets frustrated with another and another until finally there is a "blow-up" and the day starts in an uproar. That golden moment has been lost.

We can seize the golden moments because God spells them out. He tells us exactly what they are. It is going to take God's help, God's grace, and a disciplined life. But think of the dividends of a happy, joyous, wonderful home life where parents have fulfilled their responsibility and have seized the golden moments in life.

We hear so much today about children with problems. I am sorry, but someone needs to be addressing the parents. Wherever you are in this process, in this age development, and whatever your failures may be, ask the Lord to help you start right there to change things.

Let me add this footnote. Get all crudeness out of your Christian home. Christians should not talk crudely. Christian people should not have any of that in their language. I hear little children using crude terms, and they have learned them from listening to adults.

We live in a world of over six billion people and not everyone has the opportunity to live in the land where we live, and certainly not everyone in this land has the opportunity to attend a Bible-believing, Bible-preaching church. Many families will live and die and never hear one word of instruction concerning the Christian life.

I am not a child; I am a grown man with grandchildren. But these are still golden moments for me. When I sit in my home, may God teach me how precious those moments are. When I walk by the way, when I care for my daily responsibilities, may

I realize how precious they are. When I go to bed at night, it is a golden moment. When I rise in the morning to live another day, to offer my life a living sacrifice to Christ anew and afresh, I have a golden moment. This is the way God intends for life to be lived. Seize every golden moment in your home!

Home Work

♦ Make your home the safest, sweetest place on earth for your children.

♦ Enjoy eating meals together as a family.

♦ Share conversations together about the goodness of God and your love for one another.

♦ Let your children help you do things around the house and use these activities as loving, teaching times.

♦ Establish a regular time for children to go to bed.

♦ Allow no arguing, harsh words, or heavy conversation at bedtime; make it a time of peace in the house.

♦ Kneel at your child's bedside and read a Bible story each night.

♦ Have a right attitude in the morning-be pleasant and greet your children pleasantly.

♦ Make preparations for the morning on the night before.

♦ Read God's Word and pray together as a family every morning.

♦ Get all crudeness out of your Christian home.

♦ Seize every golden moment in your home!

*"Evening, and morning, and at noon,
will I pray, and cry aloud: and he
shall hear my voice."*

Psalm 55:17

Chapter Thirteen

Family Evenings With God

 n Psalm 55, we find one of the open secrets to victory in the Christian life.

Our daily schedule must be conformed to God's order. This will cause some disturbance. But remember, in order to change the future, the present must be disturbed.

Are you weary? Do you know there must be a better way to make the most of your days? Let us be completely open to the instruction we find in God's Word and seek the Lord for power to change what must be changed.

Psalm 55 is a testimony from the heart of King David in which he goes to the Lord pleading with God for help. He asks

God to give ear to his prayer. He asks God to attend unto him and to give him wings like a dove to fly away and be at rest.

David sought escape. The only place of escape from this world is in the bosom of God. We escape by meeting the Lord and communing with Him. This is the way God has designed the Christian life. As Christians, we are in this world, but not of this world. We can find in Him the rest that we need.

The Bible says in Psalm 55:16-17,

> *As for me, I will call upon God; and the LORD shall save me. Evening, and morning, and at noon, will I pray, and cry aloud: and he shall hear my voice.*

Note very carefully the order that God gives us here, *"evening, and morning, and at noon."* With only a casual reading of the fifty-fifth Psalm, one might pass over the seventeenth verse. Why did God not tell David to say, "Morning, noon, and evening will I cry aloud: and he shall hear my voice"?

What we have here is not simply a statement that David makes during a difficult time in his life. This is the Word of God. Make special note of the order, *"evening, and morning, and at noon."* God has a great principle here for us: the day should begin in the evening.

In Genesis 1:5 the Lord says, *"And the evening and the morning were the first day."* In Genesis 1:8 the Bible says at the conclusion of the verse, *"And the evening and the morning were the second day."* In verse thirteen the Bible says, *"And the evening and the morning were the third day."* In verse nineteen the Bible says, *"And the evening and the morning were the fourth day."* In verse twenty-three the Bible says, *"And the evening and the morning were the fifth day."* Then, in Genesis 1:31 the Bible says at the closing part of the verse, *"And the evening and the morning were the sixth day."*

In the Garden of Eden, God established this principle of beginning the day, not in the morning, but in the evening. We learn from this passage that the day did not start in the morning.

Luke 6:12 tells us, *"And it came to pass in those days, that he went out into a mountain to pray, and continued all night in prayer to God."* Jesus Christ started praying in the evening and continued all night in prayer.

John 1:35-39 says,

> *Again the next day after John stood, and the two of his disciples; and looking upon Jesus as he walked, he saith, Behold the Lamb of God! And the two disciples heard him speak, and they followed Jesus. Then Jesus turned, and saw them following, and saith unto them, What seek ye? They said unto him, Rabbi, (which is to say, being interpreted, Master,) where dwellest thou? He saith unto them, Come and see. They came and saw where he dwelt, and abode with him that day: for it was about the tenth hour.*

What is the tenth hour? The Jew had a twelve-hour day. It began at six in the morning, and the first hour was completed at seven. The second hour was completed at eight, the third hour at nine, the fourth hour at ten, the fifth hour at eleven, the sixth hour at noon, the seventh hour at one, the eighth hour at two, the ninth hour at three, the tenth hour at four, the eleventh hour at five, and the twelfth hour at six in the evening.

The tenth hour was four in the afternoon. At four o'clock these two disciples came in contact with the Son of God. Notice the questions in these verses. In verse thirty-eight Jesus Christ turns to them and asks the question, *"What seek ye?"* In return, they asked Him the question, *"Where dwellest thou?"* Think of these questions: "What do you want?" and "Where do you live?"

Did you ever think about why they had to ask the Lord Jesus where He lived? The Son of Man had no place to lay His head. They would not have had to ask where Peter or James lived, but they had to ask where Jesus Christ lived. He said to them, *"Come and see."*

After the Lord told them to *"Come and see," "they came and saw where he dwelt, and abode with him."* The Bible does not say that they abode in a certain place, but that they abode with a certain Person.

> *The only place of escape from this world is in the bosom of God.*

Life is not about places, but about the Person of Jesus Christ. I thought years ago when I came to this place that I was coming to East Tennessee. However, I was not primarily coming to East Tennessee; I was coming to God as I followed His leading in my life. Our heavenly Father bears us on eagles' wings and brings us unto Himself. The Lord wants us to abide in Him.

These two disciples had fellowship with God the Son at four in the afternoon and then spent the evening with God.

So many Christians have the order wrong–racing in the morning, racing through the day, closing down at night. If we are going to follow the clear teaching of the Bible, our day must begin in the evening. We need to spend the evening with God.

Anyone would tell you that a good night's rest is absolutely essential for your health and labor. Why should we be surprised that God instructs us in His Word that before we retire for a night's rest, we need to spend the evening with God?

Those without Christ will never understand "spending the evening with God." As a matter of fact, they not only have the hours of the day confused, they have the days of the week confused also. The world considers Sunday to be the last day of the week.

To the world, Sunday is the day to be consumed on self. They consider it the last day of the week before they have to "get back in the grind." The world's week starts with Monday as the first day, Tuesday as the second day, Wednesday as the third day, Thursday as the fourth day, Friday as the fifth day, Saturday as the sixth day, and Sunday as the seventh day.

Many disobedient churches are now offering "busy" people an opportunity to come on Saturday nights for a worship service. I would not call it a worship service, though they may refer to it as a "Jesus celebration" or a "praise service." It is casually committed, so-called Christianity and not what we find in the Bible.

Everyone knows that nothing strong can be built with a casual approach. Can you imagine an olympic athlete being told, "Just plug in when you find time"? Can you imagine two people in a marriage saying, "Just plug in every once in a while"?

> *Life is not about places, but about the Person of Jesus Christ.*

God has clearly taught us in His Word that the first day of the week, Sunday, is the Lord's Day and that we are to come aside to worship Him on the Lord's Day. We are to meet with God, abide with Him, and worship Him *"in spirit and in truth."* We need to prepare our hearts for the rest of the week. We should bring our gifts and hearts to God on the Lord's Day.

Why are we commanded to do all of this on the first day? We do this because it is the day of Christ's resurrection. We rejoice in our risen Savior and ascended Lord who ever liveth at the right hand of the Father making intercession for us. As Christians, we must not get caught up in the perverted order of things that the world uses.

If we are going to have victory in our Christian lives, we must take this approach to the day. The day will not begin in the morning. It will begin in the evening. In other words, there should be a time in the evening when we meet the Lord and abide in Him. True, we are constantly abiding in Him, but we must deliberately set time aside for evenings with God.

This does not sound like what is going on in most of our lives. Most homes, even Christian homes, have the television going in the evenings. People rush in, and family members go different directions in the evening. There is a tremendous amount of noise in the house during the evenings. People run late for everything in the evening. Finally exhausted, everyone falls asleep with little or no thought to planning and preparing for the night. Hurry becomes the scourge of the morning. Off they go into the day, without God and His Word. Christians who live this way never show forth Christ as they should. This problem could be cared for by giving the evenings to God. Let each of us face this matter and seek the Lord for victory.

The "night life" has become a term commonly recognized as a time to indulge oneself in the pleasures of this world. Before people made so much of the night and tried to cram so much in, they knew the value of the evening. Think a moment about your evenings. What do you do in your evenings? Do you get settled down or do you get wound up? Does your life get quieter? Is there calm or confusion?

Seeking to please the Lord in our homes means that specific things should be found in our evenings with God.

EVENING FAITH

In the evenings with God we will find faith. Faith is *"looking unto Jesus"* (Hebrews 12:2). Faith reflects on the activity of the day, believing that God's hand was in everything. Faith delivers all the day's activities to God, resting in the Lord and knowing that God is in control, not only of this universe, but of our lives. We have soul rest by trusting in the Lord. The Lord has cared for us through the day and will watch over us through the night. In the evenings with God we find faith.

EVENING GRATITUDE

In the evenings with God we find gratitude. The Lord has seen us through the day and allowed us to be together with our loved ones. Christians who live by themselves should realize that they are not alone; they are alone with God.

In the evenings with God, we will find gratitude because when we commune with the Lord and abide in Him, we cannot grumble and gripe about everything we do not have. We will be grateful to God for His blessings.

Faith delivers all the day's activities to God, resting in the Lord and knowing that God is in control, not only of this universe, but of our lives.

EVENING BIBLE READING

In the evenings with God we will find Bible reading. Keep your Bible handy. Develop a plan for reading your Bible systematically. Of course, we must allow the Lord an opportunity to break into our routine if need be and lead us to other passages of Scripture. The evening is a good time to read a designated Bible story. God speaks to us through His Word. Meet the Lord in His Word in the evening.

EVENING FELLOWSHIP

In the evenings with God there should be fellowship. If there is fellowship between you and the Lord, that is wonderful! If there is fellowship between you, the Lord, and other family members, that is wonderful! Let there be fellowship. This means to find out what you have in common. Do you know the Lord? Do you know your family?

Turn the television off; put the books down; lay aside the newspaper. In this evening with God, find fellowship with God and family members. Find out what you have in common. Talk to one another. This is vital. Let your heart be quiet and enjoy fellowship in the evening with God and your family.

EVENING TESTIMONY

In these evenings with God there should be testimony. If we are not careful, we will find ourselves dragging about, complaining, and being disgusted with what we did not accomplish. In these evenings with God, let there be testimony. Praise the Lord; give glory to God.

There is no doubt that the praises of God's people, testifying and talking about the goodness of God, will drive the Devil far away.

EVENING PRAYER

In the evenings with God there should be prayer. Touch the loved ones in your home; hold their hands; pray together. Our homes should be serene places, not battlefields. So much of the blame for the unrest in our homes can be traced to our failure to properly assign the right emphasis to the evenings.

Some may say, "I have my favorite television program to watch" or "I have the news to catch up on." Turn the television off or put it in the closet. We all have more information than we know what to do with already. We live in an information age. We do not suffer from a lack of information; we suffer from a lack of truth.

Make the evenings a time of prayer. You do not have to pray lengthy prayers. Just get your heart quiet before God.

EVENING MEDITATION

Evenings with God should include meditation. The right kind of music in your home will help this meditation. Much of the music that is called Christian is not Christian music.

There is a difference between the world's music and the Lord's music. The world's music is not going to quiet your heart and allow you to praise God for His goodness. Call to mind the wonderful Word of God and praise Him for who He is.

> *So much of the blame for the unrest in our homes can be traced to our failure to properly assign the right emphasis to the evenings.*

One of the rules in our home is that we do not read things at night like news reports, news magazines, or other heavy things. Instead, the things we read in the evening should be about the Lord and His people. Make it a practice in your home to read biographies of God's choice servants.

Do not read anything hard or heavy in the evenings. This will enable you to think about the goodness of God. Dwell on God's blessings and provisions.

When you have an evening with God, you can lay your head on the pillow and get a good night's rest and have a much better start for the next day.

Bring your family together and tell them that you are going to start having evenings with God. If you have some sort of entertainment in your home, put a time limit on it. Make time to be together. It does not have to be a long time, but in our homes we must make time for faith, gratitude, testimony, fellowship, prayer, meditation, and Bible reading.

It would be a blessed thing if God's people all across this land would stop in the evening to meet God, meditate on His goodness, read His Word, and pray together.

"Evening, and morning, and at noon, will I pray . . . and he shall hear my voice."

Home Work

♦ Each evening, show faith in God by speaking of His care throughout the day and His promise to watch over you in the night.

♦ Each evening, express your gratitude to God for His blessings.

♦ Each evening, meet the Lord in His Word.

♦ Each evening, set aside time to fellowship with the Lord and with other family members.

♦ Each evening, share testimonies of the goodness of God and praise Him.

♦ Each evening, pray together with your family.

♦ Each evening, meditate on the Lord and His Word.

♦ Bring your family together and determine to have evenings with God.

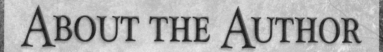

ABOUT THE AUTHOR

Clarence Sexton is the pastor of the Temple Baptist Church and founder of Crown College in Knoxville, Tennessee. He has written more than twenty books and booklets. He speaks in conferences throughout the United States and has conducted training sessions for pastors and Christian workers in several countries around the world. He and his wife, Evelyn, have been married for thirty-six years. They have two grown sons and six grandchildren. For more information about the ministry of Clarence Sexton, visit our website at www.faithforthefamily.com.

OTHER BOOKS BY CLARENCE SEXTON

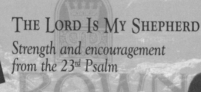

THE LORD IS MY SHEPHERD

Strength and encouragement from the 23rd Psalm

EARNESTLY CONTEND FOR THE FAITH

Encouraging boldness in the Christian life in these perilous times